Choral
CHARISMA

Singing with Expression

by
Tom Carter

Published by
Santa Barbara Music Publishing, Inc.
Post Office Box 41003
Santa Barbara, California, 93140

First Printing: January, 2005
Second Printing: February, 2006, revised
Third Printing: September, 2008

Carter, Tom

Choral Charisma
Singing with Expression

ISBN: 0-9648071-5-7

Acknowledgments

In chronological order...

Thank you to Jack Carey, my high school choral director, and Lesley Saladen, my 9th grade English teacher—both of whom teamed up to direct the musicals. You had a formative effect on my life and I will always be grateful.

Thank you to Charlene Archibeque, my Choraliers director, Masters advisor, and steadfast supporter. Your asking me to coach the Choraliers in 1989 planted the seeds for this project, and your conducting is a constant inspiration.

Thank you to all the students I have taught, the actors I have directed, and the colleagues I have learned from. You have all contributed to my growth as a teacher, director, and human being. I am rich with fond memories because of you.

Thank you to Susan Aiken, my partner and reader—your thoughts and insights made the book *much* better. You have had a similar impact on the author throughout the years—without your loving support, I would not have been capable of even beginning this project.

Thank you to Michael Pease, also my reader. Your wise, perceptive, and oh-so-detailed comments have helped immeasurably. The fact that you made the time to help me is appreciated even more.

Thank you to all the choral directors and singers I have had the pleasure of coaching. Your insights, comments, and enthusiasm inspired me to write this book. I'm eternally grateful.

Thank you to all the authors whose work I have referenced and quoted. The phrase "I stand on the back of giants" could never be more apt. Your words have combined to create more substance and more interest for this reader, that's for sure!

Thank you to Leon Thurman, whose help with editing enabled the first three chapters to "aim for the bullseye." Your willingness to share your wisdom reveals a most generous spirit.

Thank you to Barbara Harlow, my publisher and editor. Your passion for the project—combined with your steely eye for detail—has resulted in a most enjoyable experience. Thank you for holding my feet to the fire, but being continually encouraging.

Introduction

On November 9, 2003, in a glorious stone church with impossibly high ceilings, I had the great pleasure of experiencing a concert performed by the UC Berkeley Choral Ensembles. Director Mark Sumner had created a wonderful evening of anti-war songs, interspersed with poems and readings done by individual choir members. His 160 singers (combined) did a spectacular job with the material—they felt it deeply, expressing themselves individually and collectively in such a way that I was spellbound, and deeply moved. It wasn't until the concert was over that I realized I was in pain from sitting on a hard wooden pew for two-and-a-half hours. When talking to some audience members after the show, I realized I was not alone in my appreciation. "The singers were so 'into it,' almost like rock singers. Their faces were so alive and expressive!" was the response of one gentleman. Another audience member said, "Wow! There was something so different about that concert. But in a good way!" These words were proverbial music to my ears, because I had worked with these singers at their retreat and during their dress rehearsal, helping them to create just this kind of experience for themselves and the audience members. To say that I was pleased would be an understatement. The truth is that I am ecstatic to be offering a process that helps singers and directors create more memorable and exciting performances.

While people have used vocal music as a way to connect on a deep, human, "soul" level for millennia, this book introduces a specific approach that demystifies the "soul connection" process, empowering singers and directors to connect to the music, and the audience, with passion and poignancy. And while it's true that there are many wonderful choirs out there, even the best choirs are capable of a deeper connection, one that will engender more exciting and engaging performances.

The self-test that follows will give you a sense of your choir's current level of connection and expression.

Self-Test

Evaluate your experience on a scale of 1 through 5,
with 1 being never, 3 being sometimes, and 5 being always.

1	2	3	4	5
Never		**Sometimes**		**Always**

During Rehearsals...

1. ___ Do singers talk to each other while you are trying to address an individual, a section, or the whole group?
2. ___ Do you continue to address the group, even though some people are talking or clearly not paying attention?
3. ___ Do some choir members make jokes at other members' expense, or put each other down?
4. ___ Do you get angry or lose your temper?
5. ___ Are there singers who don't sing out?
6. ___ Are there singers who seem to resist attempts to get them to be expressive?
7. ___ Have you found rationalizations for the choir's lack of expression: they're too young, too old, not religious enough, a church choir, all boys, teenage girls?

During Performances...

8. ___ Do individual singers' faces look the same, regardless of the music being sung?
9. ___ Do their bodies look stiff?
10. ___ Do their heads stay still?
11. ___ Do they have a seemingly limited range of facial expressions?
12. ___ Do they rarely smile or lift their eyebrows?
13. ___ Do their faces or bodies communicate one thing while the music communicates another?
14. ___ Do they look like they're worried, depressed, or bored?
15. ___ Do you look at the choir and wish they could be more expressive?
16. ___ Do your audiences have unexpressive faces as they experience the choir?

After Performances...

17. ___ Do your audience members talk mostly about the sound of the group, as opposed to the experience they had when the group was singing?

While there is no definitive chart to analyze your results, perhaps the process itself led you to some interesting musings. Where do your current skills place you on the continuum of choral expression? As you take a look at how you evaluated your singing or your choir, I invite you to consider the possibilities for personal or professional growth.

How will this book be helpful in the growth process? Singers and directors have presented terrific concerts for centuries. However, while compelling and vibrant singing has been around longer than the oldest cathedrals of Europe, the process described in this book is a relatively fresh one, especially as applied to choral singing.

You might have heard directors say things like, "More joy here, please!" or "Your face is not communicating what the music is saying. Show it on your face." You probably know singers who said to themselves, "Look angry now, the lyrics are angry lyrics." They might even have "looked angry" at that point. Many directors have a positive intention to communicate the music's passion and humanity. Unfortunately, the methods they use fall short—even to the degree of creating an actual disconnect between the singer, the soul of the music, and the audience. There is a more direct path, one that leads to truthful connection and truly expressive singing.

To understand the origins and underpinnings of this approach, it may be helpful to look at my background. For the past thirty years I've been a classically trained singer who has enjoyed singing in many choirs. I've also been an actor and stage director, one who got a BA in Drama Education to pursue a career in teaching. During the past twenty years I have been a teacher of English, Drama, and Speech at the middle and high school levels, and a stage director at all levels. In 1987, I enrolled in San Jose State University to work with Dr. Charlene Archibeque and sing with her wonderful Choraliers. Two years later I earned my Masters degree in Music Theatre. Those two words, "music" and "theatre," capture my approach to the work, for I apply a distinct theatre background to vocal and choral performance. To analyze the conductor's role, I use my understanding of teaching and stage directing.

Here is the chain of events that led to the writing of this book. As I sang and attended concerts over the last 30 years, my "teacher/director" self discovered a very exciting area of potential. Often in a choral performance, the soul of the music doesn't make it to the soul of the audience. The composer pours their heart and soul into the music, then the director pours their heart and soul into it—connecting to it, knowing exactly how they are going to conduct it so that it is beautiful and exciting. Rehearsals see lots of sweat flying as the director does their best to communicate their vision to the choir. The singers work hard to blend, sing in tune, and bring the director's interpretation alive. Then the concert happens and the audience members are impressed. "What beautiful music! Such control! Listen to those sopranos!" However (and this is critical) while they are impressed, they are not moved. Why not? Because the most important "heart and soul connection" often hasn't been developed fully enough. Whose connection is that? *That connection belongs solely to the singer.* The collective audience can only be moved deeply if the singer's personal connection to text and music is compelling and complete. In such a concert, all involved would be transported to a celebration of shared humanity, thanks to the singers sharing their authentic selves with the audience, the director, and each other.

Because I got so excited by the potential of this work, 15 years ago I started to coach the San Jose State Choraliers, working with them before important concerts or competitions. This work seemed a natural progression, since my passion had always been to help actors and singers connect personally and powerfully with the material, creating memorable experiences for themselves and their audiences. So, for the last decade I have been doing more of this type of work with directors, choirs, and soloists, and the process has been extremely rewarding. When singers connect to the text and music, their faces are alive and expressive, their singing is dynamic and nuanced, and, most significantly, their connection draws the audience into the heart and soul of the music.

Choral Charisma is written to the choral director, but is also intended for singers (of all types), voice teachers, and stage directors. In this book, I present my approach to expressive singing, and describe how it can be implemented. In addition, I discuss how directors can create an atmosphere of safety and security—an atmosphere that supports full expression. And while the book describes a comprehensive approach, it is a "friendly" guide, one that you can hopefully learn from readily but enjoy at the same time.

About six weeks before that profoundly moving concert discussed at the opening of this introduction, I had the pleasure of working with many of those UC Berkeley singers for the first time. After the workshop, the director emailed, "You helped raise our performance bar, and the thought of its potential is almost overwhelming."

Here's hoping that this book will help you do the same, and more.

Dedication

I dedicate this book to the memory of three special people: my parents, Tom and Terry Carter, and former student Mandy Hafleigh, each of whom loved the arts and supported personal expression in all its forms.

By extension, this book is written for all moms, dads, sons, and daughters of this our human family, as we each endeavor to find our most truthfully connected voice. May we all sing with joy and abandon!

The following is a poem written by my grandfather when my dad was an infant. It speaks of similar hopes.

To My Boy
by Pel Carter

Last night the clock struck midnight
From the steeple near at hand;
I was wide awake and sleepless
In a far—and stranger's—land.

I counted sheep—yes, backward!
I pictured waves of blue;
But sleep was far from coming—
My thoughts were all of you.

My mind raced back to meet you
Over many weary miles
I saw you gently sleeping—
Your mouth turned up in smiles.

Your tousled head was nestled
On your mother's loving arm
And I whispered
"Dear Lord, bless them
And keep them safe from harm."

Just then my eyes grew weary,
I slept till break of day.
An angel seemed to stand nearby
And I thought I heard him say,

"Choose now, you father, for the lad
That boy you love so true!
The years are swiftly passing
And it's mostly up to you.

What will you that I give the boy
When he is grown—ere long?
Great riches? Strength? Or Learning?
Or in his heart—a song?"

Great riches!
Well—they're not so much
When peace is not your goal!
Gold and silver are not balm
for a tired and life-seared soul.

Strong body? Sure, that's wonderful
But something soon forgot
When you're frowning at your loved ones
And happiness is not.

Learning? Yes, that's best so far,
But what's that to a song?
Or just a little smile, maybe,
When everything is wrong?

What do I wish for that boy of mine?
When he is grown so big?
I want to hear him whistling
Even though he's flunked in Trig.

Latin, Greek, and History!
Wealth and a body strong!
All these I want, Dear Lord, for him
But—first and last—a song.

Table of Contents

1

Safety First

Not a gift of a cow, nor a gift of land, nor yet a gift of food, is so
important as the gift of safety, which is declared to
be the great gift among all gifts in this world.

Panchatantra (C. 5ᵗʰ C.), I, Tr. Franklin Edgerton

Fully expressive choral singing requires a particular kind of environment in
which to thrive. This test will help you get a feel for your choir's environment,
letting you know what its strengths and opportunities might be.

Self-Test for Directors
Adaptable for Singers

T F The singers in your choir seem to like you.

T F They are very responsive to you, doing what you ask quickly and
earnestly.

T F Everyone listens respectfully whenever anyone, be it you or a singer, "has the
floor."

T F The singers share their thoughts readily and respectfully.

T F They usually treat each other with kindness.

T F Positive energy is the norm in rehearsal.

T F You care about each singer in your choir.

T F You rarely experience frustration or anger.

T F You are happy with the way you "discipline."

T F The singers would say that your "discipline" methods are very
effective.

T F You laugh at yourself easily.

T F Your mood is usually positive, even if your rehearsals are fast-paced.

T F You are rarely sarcastic or authoritarian.

T F You feel comfortable as the choir's leader.

T F The singers respect you.

T F You are aware when you start to feel fear, anger, or insecurity, and
you manage your thoughts and actions accordingly.

If you answered "true" to all of these statements, your choir probably has an atmosphere which is conducive to expressive singing. If you answered "false" to one or more questions, there is more you can do to create that safe environment. Chapter One explores practical methods to help develop Safety, as well as the philosophy behind them—within the first chapter is the core of the "choral charisma" process.

> Without safety, a choir will never be fully expressive.
> It's that simple.

A Tale of Two Choirs

It was the best of atmospheres, it was the worst of atmospheres.

The following examples are melded from my experiences doing workshops with many different choirs.

High School Choir #1

As the students talk and laugh with one another, the teacher says, "You have 30 seconds until the bell rings. Please get in formation on the risers." They do so. Hardly anyone talks, and those who do speak quietly. There is a feeling of joyful expectation in the room. When the teacher walks in front of them all eyes are on her, and all mouths are closed. The teacher greets them, then introduces me. She gives them directions that they follow with ease and grace. As they warm up, every student is fully engaged in the process. "We're now going to sing *You Are the New Day* for Tom. Change to the proper formation, please." They do so and nobody talks. When they get to their positions, they look right at the teacher and await her cue. After singing, they generously allow me to work with them on some new techniques. Given a chance to sing again—but this time with more expression—they do so, embracing freshly introduced skills with a confident vulnerability. After they finish singing, they share their thoughts readily and with enthusiasm.

"That was so much more fun!"
"It gave me something to think about besides the notes."
"I was a lot more emotional!"

So many wanted to share that I didn't have time to call on them all.

Impressive, to say the least. During the entire workshop the singers were kind, polite, respectful, and gracious towards each other and towards the adults in the room. And most significantly, they were extremely open in their willingness to share and risk honestly expressing themselves—both in their comments and their singing. Contrast that with…

High School Choir #2

The bell rings. The students gradually settle into their seats, still talking (some raucously). The teacher waits a moment, then addresses the group. "Good morning, class. A couple of housekeeping notes first. Girls, it's the long outfits for the photo shoot, right? And remember, party afterword at Pizza Palace." There was an additional minute of this sort of thing, but you get the idea. "Now today we have a special guest who is going to work with us on stage presence." And the teacher gave "Mr. Carter" a very kind introduction for another 45 seconds or so.

Looking at what the teacher did, there's no cause for concern. It's what some of the students did, and what this teacher did *not* do, that reveals the problem. From the time the teacher began to address the group, to the end of his introduction of me, there was a constant buzz from the back two rows. About 12 of the 60 singers were having their own smirk-filled discussions, commenting on the people and events in the classroom, and creating a grating undertone of negative energy that sawed right through the teacher's remarks. Papers were shuffled, throats were "cleared" (with words disguised therein). One student even crumpled a piece of paper and lobbed the three-pointer into the wastebasket, the "ball" soaring over the heads of half the choir. *Remarkably, the teacher didn't do a thing about any of this, acting as if the disrespectful behavior wasn't happening.* Consequently, the atmosphere in that rehearsal room was an odd mixture of intimidation, denial, and unmistakable tension.

I knew that this behavior had to be addressed in order for the choir to have even the slightest willingness to sing with expression. It was terrifying enough for the singers to volunteer—it took a full 15 minutes before anyone was brave enough to share even the shortest comment about their own experience. Every singer there knew that any sign of vulnerability would make them targets for the poachers in the back rows. The choir's atmosphere had to be changed, and quickly. Otherwise, nothing I would do for the next 90 minutes would convince them that it was safe to risk singing with passion and honesty.

Thinking it best to confront the issue directly, I addressed the behavior—asserting the points that you'll encounter in this first chapter—and laid the responsibility for supportive behavior squarely on the group. Every time the behavior returned, I countered, holding the singers accountable for every word and action. The 12 singers did all they could to maintain dominance, but the rest of the class slowly began to stand up to them, saying "Sh!" and "Support!" during each new act of subterfuge. Eventually there was an overwhelming solidarity that shut down and even converted the intimidators, and a fledgling expressive choir was born.

The moral of our epic? Any choir can be an expressive choir, but it must be a *safe* choir first.

High Expectations

Respect and Support for All

The best way to create a safe choral environment is to have high expectations of respectful and supportive behavior. These expectations apply to everybody, including the director. If the director treats the singers with rudeness and insensitivity, it will not matter how well the singers treat each other. Such a director will never have a fully expressive choir, no matter how hard they try.

If a director treats the singers well, and insists that they treat each other well, the vast majority of singers will feel safe. And because they feel safe, they will also be willing to be vulnerable. Their vulnerability, in turn, will allow them to connect to the music at a deeper level, eventually leading to passionate expression. Common sense and your own experience will probably confirm this fact: We are more likely to risk expressing our authentic and complete selves if we feel safe doing so. Science verifies this as well. As author and co-editor Leon Thurman writes in *Book One* of *Bodymind & Voice: Foundations of Voice Education,* brain research has shown the following:

> People who feel safe while engaging in meaningful activity learn more effectively, think more clearly, and have much more fun!

Thurman elaborates that unthreatened people have access to feelings like joy, satisfaction, and ecstasy. When we feel unsafe, we are wary and constricted—part of us is on constant alert for the need to "fight, flee, or freeze." In an unsafe choir, singers using these defense mechanisms might argue with the director, quit the choir, or (most significantly) remain passive, unengaged, and uncommitted.

For me there is no choice. Give me safety or give me…safety! An unsafe choir will not enable the singers, the director, or the audience to experience ALL the wonderful things that choral music has to offer. A safe choir will.

Help Singers Support Each Other

Let's take a look at how the director can set the tone of safety from day one, using the school choir as model. Start off with a short talk on Support addressing the following points:

- Singing requires singers to express themselves in an honest and vulnerable way.
- This can not be done in an atmosphere of judgment, ridicule, or teasing.
- The most exciting singing is done in an atmosphere of Support.
- This vital ingredient is created when all members of the group treat each other as equals, all deserving respect and dignity.

This might be your statement to the choir:

> If you don't support the other people in the group, they won't feel safe enough to "go for it," to sing out, to risk making a mistake or being vulnerable. They won't trust that you want them to succeed or be their best. Because of this, they will always hold back, and never express themselves fully in the music. They won't let you or the audience see their souls, their humanity. So, support is a big deal. Without it, your singing will be uninspired, your performances will never touch your audiences, and choir will never be as fun or engaging as it could be.

It also is instructive for you (the director) to give an example of what constitutes unsupportive behavior, and explain how it will hurt the group.

> Steve is auditioning for a solo, and Maria thinks he sounds terrible. Maria doesn't say anything, but she looks at the person next to her and does this... (Make a face which communicates the clear message, "Yuck! He sounds terrible!") Negative energy floods into the room immediately, and makes it an unsafe place for people to express themselves. Even though it might seem like no big deal, someone making a "little" face like that can do big harm. Anybody that happens to notice Maria's face *definitely* gets the idea that keeping their voice to themselves is the safest thing to do in this choir. If Steve sees Maria make that face, you can only imagine how badly he might feel, and how reluctant he would be to do anything that would risk more judgment or shame.

The singers can then brainstorm ideas of unsupportive and supportive behavior while working in pairs or small groups. After a few minutes, ask for volunteers to share with the full group. Here are some possible results of their discussion:

Unsupportive Behavior

- Talking while the teacher is addressing an individual or the group.
- Talking when a singer has the floor.
- Speaking negatively about someone behind their back.
- Passing notes while someone has the floor.
- Arriving late and unprepared.
- Being mean, sarcastic, or insulting.
- Acting in such a way that the person thinks you don't like them.
- Making fun of someone.
- Avoiding someone who wants to talk to you.
- Teasing, because someone might take it the wrong way. Or the "right" way. (Which is why I discourage teasing of any kind.)
- Moving around a lot, or making distracting noises when the attention should be focused on someone else.
- Acting out so that people pay lots of attention to you.
- Wanting someone to do badly or to feel bad about themselves.

Supportive Behavior

- Focusing on whomever has the floor, reacting to them in such a way that they know you're really listening (This includes nodding, smiling, laughing, frowning if you don't understand—this active listening is the opposite of staring blankly.)
- Arriving early or on time and being prepared.
- Smiling at people when they look at you.
- Thinking ahead of the consequences of your behavior, then only making supportive choices.
- Looking for ways to help people, then doing so.
- Leaving your troubles outside the door so that your negative energy doesn't affect others.
- Applauding someone with sincerity.
- Congratulating someone if they do a good job.
- Helping the other people in the group to do well.
- Helping each other grow as confident, expressive beings.

Why Pairs or Small Groups?

A student once told me that she never spoke in any of her middle school classes because she didn't feel comfortable sharing her opinion in front of the whole group. I don't know about you, but when I'm in a faculty meeting and I want to speak, I often have to give myself a major pep talk *"Come on, you've got a really good point! Just ignore your pounding heart and sweaty palms!"* Public speaking is one of America's top fears, even topping heights, snakes, and death. Your singers fear it, too, and the more opportunities you can give them for safer expression, the better.

> **Participating in small groups will feel safer to many in the choir.** More people will readily contribute to the discussion, expressing themselves with relative ease. The main reason for this is that people are more likely to risk being vulnerable sharing with a few peers than with the whole group.

> **Small groups develop expressive confidence.** Each singer gets a chance to practice in a safe "small pond." This helps them develop personal confidence and trust in their peers, both of which will be necessary as the invitations for expression get more intense.

> **The small-group process values each member and strengthens overall cohesiveness.** Giving them the opportunity to share and interact with each other validates the importance of each individual singer, develops the feeling of community, and helps each singer feel they belong.

> **Small groups facilitate more meaningful learning.** For most of us, actively engaging in the process yields better educational results than merely listening or watching.

The time for the first teacher-led group discussion is much later, once the safe atmosphere has been established. Pair and group work is always the better option if you can incorporate it into the rehearsal. It works well to ask singers to "share with the person next to them," and you'll consistently get more total group expression if you do so. However, if you can't do this, asking for a few comments from volunteers early in the process is not going to cause major harm—and it will often give you a sense of the current level of safety in the group. If all hands shoot up and all faces are beaming, the singers probably feel safe!

Warning: Unless you know for a fact that every singer feels comfortable speaking in public, and each singer trusts and supports every other singer, refrain from calling on individuals. Your attempt to keep the rehearsal moving, or to encourage certain singers to participate more, will create an atmosphere of fear and tension. Don't let the fact that this is a common teaching technique lead you astray—this practice does not create safety within the group. It's better for you to deal with your own discomfort when that silent moment hits than to try and "pull" responses from the unwilling.

Humanistic Discipline

Once the sharing is over, let the group know that you will respond to un-supportive behavior, reinforcing the safe environment whenever necessary. This is helpful for most choirs with singers of high school age or younger as it reassures them that you will be an effectual leader.

Since the singer's safety is built on emotional support, your "disciplining" needs to do more than just control behavior. In order to develop a safe atmosphere, you need to honor the shared humanity of both singer and director. The more you engage the choir members as equals, without sham-ing or punishing them from a superior status position, the more everyone will benefit. Here are some examples of Humanistic Discipline.

If someone is acting in an unsupportive manner, gently but firmly say "Support, please," without even looking at the responsible party.

Address the singers directly, asking them to support you or their peers. "Rob, could you please support a little more?" And move right on.

Address them directly, sharing the impact their behavior is having on you. "Jasmine, I'm noticing that it's really hard for me to stay focused on helping the altos when you're talking. Would you support us, please?"

Spend a few moments helping the singer figure out what's going on. "Danny, I've got to stop for a minute and ask you if you know what's behind your unsupportive behavior today. Can you sense the impact you're having on the group? I've got to tell you, I get nervous whenever you open your mouth because I'm afraid of whose feelings you might hurt next. Is there anything we can do to help you with this?" Saying this sincerely and with loving intent can work wonders to build trust.

Speaking kindly and firmly, ask the singer to move to a different seat. If their behavior just won't stop, ask them firmly but lovingly to go outside until they are ready to come back in and support the group.

Your use of humanistic discipline will strengthen the choir's sense of com-munity, humanize your relationship with them, and help the individuals take responsibility for their growth as respectful and aware human beings.

Now, while you might want to include consequences like parent/teacher conferences or eviction from the choir, these may never occur. In twenty years of working with people aged eight to twenty, I never needed to take those steps. A great irony here is that people are much more likely to "behave" if they are treated as equals. When leaders see discipline as a "Me versus Them" power struggle, the "subordinates" often act out. In choirs with this sort of dynamic, singers often misbehave, refusing to act respectfully when they are being disrespected themselves.

Another way to earn singers' respect is to deal with most disciplinary consequences yourself—this builds the singers' trust in you much more readily than if you cede responsibility to an administrator. Obviously, some extreme situations involving physical danger should be dealt with by an administrator or the police. Your students will be grateful to you for doing what was necessary in those instances to maintain a safe environment.

Another approach to overall "discipline" is to empower the singers to come up with the guidelines themselves through a democratic and collaborative process. Once these guidelines are determined, the group establishes what happens when someone "breaks a rule." This system can be challenging to implement to everyone's satisfaction, but when it works it can be empowering for the singers, and freeing for the director.

Respect Starts with Identity

To develop a caring community where each is known, valued, and respected, every person in the group (especially the director) needs to quickly learn everyone else's names. Do this as soon as possible following the talk on support. When you know their names, it's much easier to develop a caring rapport which enables you to know them as human beings, not just singers.

While there are many "name games," the following is the most effective I've encountered. Don't let the word "games" mislead you. Learning singers' names immediately shows them respect, and earns you the same. Significantly, this exercise requires singers to risk creative expression, and support that expression in others. Because the exercise is a fun group activity, they will also be building community. While "just a game," this is a significant first foray into group creative expression. But it won't be their last.

◆ The Name Game

Everyone stands in a circle, and thinks of a descriptive word that starts with the same sound as their name. For example, "Jumping George." (It's not the letter, it's the sound.) The main guideline for the word chosen is that the person must be able to "act it out." This acting can be as basic as putting a thumb up when acting the word, "awesome," or it can be complicated and creative. It is important that there be no limits to the creativity, but no pressure to be creative, either. Any choice is great. Give the singers a fair amount of time to come up with these descriptive words and their actions, and encourage them to ask their neighbors for suggestions if they need help. Make sure everyone has a word and an action before moving on.

The actual game consists of three rounds. During the first round, each person says their name while everyone else looks at them and repeats the name. Start with yourself, then go slowly around the circle. "Tom," I would say. "Tom," they repeat.

During the second round each person says their name and the descriptive word while everyone focuses carefully and repeats. Again, slowly. "Jumping George."

In the third round the descriptive word, name, and action are combined. Everyone tries to copy exactly how the person does this. If George jumps three times, then says "Jumping George," everyone must jump three times, then say, "Jumping George."

When all have finished, ask for volunteers to try and remember everyone's descriptive words and names. If they can't remember, the person being remembered acts out their descriptive word. If that still doesn't jog the guesser's memory, the first sound is given. Then the descriptive word itself and/or the name. It's very helpful to have at least four people try to guess everyone's words and names while the rest of the singers "follow along." *Make sure that you are one of those who volunteer.*

In the days following, ask the singers to do their action for you if you forget their names. If you haven't done something like this before, you may be surprised at the fact that you can know everyone's name by the end of the second class meeting, if not at the end of the game itself (even if you teach and have a number of different groups). However, if there are more than 40 people in any individual choir whose names you don't know, get lots of sleep the night before!

Support the Singers

Be Consistent, But Kind

After the discussion about support, the singers have a clear understanding of what they need to do, and why it is so important. It is now your obligation to be vigilant for the very first examples of unsupportive behavior. And **pounce!** But since you must show and model respect for each member of the group, the way you "pounce" is critical. Let's say that the first instance of unsupportive behavior is someone saying sarcastically, "Nice high note," when a singer's voice cracks. Without even looking at the perpetrator, "pounce," saying something like this:

> Hold it, everybody! We just had some unsupportive behavior from this part of the room. Stay aware, people. Support is critical. Disrespectful behavior creeps up on you when you least expect it.

No Shame, No Blame

There is no need to risk shaming an individual by naming them (and you *will* know their name). At this point in the process, they are just beginning to learn your expectations of them, and may even be testing you to see if you really mean it. The way you treat them during this "infancy" period speaks volumes about you, has a profound impact on them, and will do much to create a strong foundation of safety.

Making an example of a specific singer here would actually undermine the process, for they will likely feel shame, and shame rarely benefits anyone. If the director shames one singer, every other singer registers *danger;* they sense that the same thing could happen to them. Some directors use shame and fear consistently to enforce discipline. The singers in such choirs may be less talkative and less disruptive, but they will also be less trusting, less vulnerable, and less expressive.

Earn Their Trust

By valuing every student in every interaction, the teacher does a HUGE amount to promote safety and support. Here are a few of the conclusions singers will draw when you discipline firmly, fairly, and consistently, but without shame.

> **You aren't one of those "clueless" teachers** who let students get away with things. Nor are you one who disciplines "selectively." You are not afraid to call students to a high standard of behavior.

You keep negative energy out of your interactions—even when disciplining. You really *do* mean it when you talk about things like support and respect.

You have self-control and a healthy sense of perspective, recognizing that we are all fallible but lovable human beings worthy of sensitive treatment—even when we "mess up." The singers can relax around you.

Individuals in the group have self-awareness and responsibility for their actions. It is important to monitor our own behavior, not because we're afraid of getting in trouble by the "Powerful and Scary Teacher," but because it is the right thing to do for the group.

Using the No Shame, No Blame technique for the first several choir meetings will further enhance their positive perceptions of you and the choir. In addition, a stated reminder of "Support!" (with no punitive or shaming look) will often get them to do so quickly and efficiently.

Get the Whole Group's Attention

The special circumstances of trying to call an entire group to "order," whether they are being supportive or not, requires special care on your part. The following methods get the group's attention while maintaining a supportive atmosphere *and* preserving the director's voice.

1. Play a "throw support to the director" phrase on the piano.

2. Raise your hand and look around the room, smiling and making eye contact. All who see you raise their hands also, stop talking, and look at you. Then, singers who see *anybody's* hand raised do the same.

3. Clap a rhythmic pattern to which the choir responds with a set pattern of their own. As they respond, they all stop talking and focus on you. (For a variation, see p. 14, "Discipline" and the Adult Choir.)

4. Stand close to one or more singers and hum a pitch. They hum the same pitch and look at you. Others hear them and do the same. Soon, the entire group will be humming and looking at you. You can move seamlessly to other warm-ups, or use this as the basis for ear-training when you designate different sections to move incrementally in pitch.

Because of your supportive treatment, the group will begin to trust and respect you. More importantly, they will gain confidence in your ability to provide a safe environment for them. The importance of this cannot be overstated.

Use a Calm, Direct Approach Once Trust is Established

Once you sense their trust in your stewardship, shift to a calm and direct approach that emphasizes the desired response. "Patricia, focus on the music, please," said calmly and with a gentle and knowing smile, will keep the positive energy intact. Chastising sarcastically with, "Patricia, stop playing with Marisol's hair! This is Choir, not a beauty salon" can unravel your previous work with Patricia and the group. Both statements may have the same behavioral consequence, but the latter will have a very different emotional impact, damaging the safe atmosphere you are working hard to create.

Avoid Too Much Control

A director's need for too much control is also detrimental to the creation of a safe atmosphere, because the singers won't feel respected. Make sure that your expectations are reasonable and fair, taking into account their inherent and equal worth as human beings. If you are concerned with their every movement, not trusting them to make responsible decisions on their own, you are probably exerting too much control. A good question to answer is, "Would you want to be treated the way that you are treating your singers?" Answer this question from the perspective of you at your current age, not you at their age. For example, adults like to be treated well. *So do fifth grade singers.* (Actually, their sense of respectful treatment is probably heightened!) So, presuming that a fifth grader likes to sit in their seat for thirty minutes at a time with both feet on the floor even though you wouldn't... Well, "that's just not fair!" This presumes an inherent inequality between you and the singer, which precludes your authentic respect for them as human beings. As James Jordan writes in *The Musician's Soul:*

> In order to make music, one must be able to meet others on the equal ground of trusting and loving.

Another way to check for over-control is to examine what they need your permission to do, and how punitive you are if they don't do it. Are you "nice" until they do something wrong, in which case you get "mean"? Must they be in their seats when the bell rings, or else? Must they turn in their homework on time, or else? Must they only leave their seats if they raise their hand, or else? Must they only leave your classroom once a week to go to the bathroom, or else? The question to ask is, "Do they obey you because you intimidate them? Or do they support you because you respect them?"

Your singers will only be responsible if you give them responsibility. They will only be trustworthy if you trust them. They will only support other singers to grow if you help them with *their* growth. And that can only happen by nurturing and valuing them, not by controlling them.

"Discipline" and the Adult Choir

Adult choirs are no different than youth choirs. Since you are a peer of the singers, it is very important to be respectful and supportive. And even though most adults are not going to "misbehave," they might be very talkative, or distracted after a long day at work.

In the video *Ready, Set, Sing!*, Jeff Johnson advocates getting the singers' attention with a clap sequence that they then repeat. Right after they've repeated it, invite their complete focus with either a hiss or movement pattern—which they then mimic. After they respond, the director claps a different pattern (which the singers repeat) then presents a new hiss or movement pattern. This can be continued for as long as deemed constructive.

Whichever methods you choose, deal with adult "discipline" issues directly, calmly, and with non-abrasive humor whenever possible. Avoid shaming and sarcasm, but if some of your negative energy slips out, take responsibility and apologize.

The Language of Empowerment

In any choir, be it comprised of adults or younger singers, one of the best ways to build a community of equals is to empower the individuals in the group. While this entire truthful connection process is about creative empowerment, there are also less creative—but equally valid—avenues of empowerment.

A great way to empower the singers is to speak to them in a way that reflects their status as creative artists. Avoid the terms, "I want" and "I need" when you address them. "I want you to give me more volume, here" or "I need more from the basses" is actually demeaning, implying that the director is the important person they need to please, and they are but minions. Instead, say something like, "Let's try that again, but this time really pump up the volume." Avoid "I" statements when you praise them, as well. Telling them "That's what I'm looking for!" when they achieve a goal will again put the focus on the director—and on the importance of making the director happy. This is a critical point. I've seen singers filled with resentment when they work with—but feel like they're working under—a director using "It's All About Me" language.

Leon Thurman feels that the content of a director's feedback can empower as well, suggesting that specific feedback is more valuable than praise. For example, saying "The tone was so much clearer when everybody matched the vowel" is much more helpful than just saying "Fantastic!" and moving on. This is not to say that words of praise have no place in the rehearsal room—when they are genuine expressions of celebration instead of attempts at manipulation, they are most welcome. Indeed, such celebrations can give directors and singers some of their greatest moments of joy. Giving specific feedback, however, allows the singers to see themselves and their process more clearly. If you celebrate ("Wow! That was incredible!") but then add specific feedback—your response becomes about them and the results of their efforts instead of how much you liked what they did. They will not only feel validated and empowered by your redirection of the focus, they will also learn at a deeper level since you are reminding them of their constructive choices. Thurman calls this "implicit, constructive praise."

Thurman also recommends that the singers give "self-perceived feedback" whereby they answer open-ended questions about their own process. Your questions like "What did you notice about that chord?" or "What changed when you were emotionally involved?" will increase their self-awareness and empower them to speak about the singing process. That is the goal. When they answer, treat every volunteer's comment with equal respect by restating it and adding your own supportive reflection. They will then know that they, and their perceptions, are valued.

While open-ended questions empower, closed questions (for which there is only one "correct" answer) can subtly disempower. Beware the "Who's Got the Right Answer?" questioning strategy—in which the director keeps calling on people until someone answers the question "correctly." While this technique may seem substantive, it creates a frustrating dynamic for the singers, fortifying their perception that the director has the power and the singers are only there to please. To prevent this insidious dynamic, keep your questions open-ended as often as you can. To direct the singers' focus to details, move from general to specific open-ended questions.

Questioning Styles

Open-ended: What did you feel that time?
Closed: What feeling should you have had that time?
General: What did you notice about the sound that time?
Specific: What did you notice when we matched vowels on "life"?

Just as your questioning style can empower the singers, so can giving them opportunities to make meaningful choices.

What would you like to work on next, the Debussy or the Ives?
What do you think, should we take a break now or barrel through?
How many like these new chairs? Should we send them back?
Which warm-ups shall we do today?
Which pieces do you want to perform this Friday?
All right. I sense that this is not your favorite piece. How many want
   to take it out of our repertoire?

Asking questions like these (and asking questions in general) makes a remarkable difference. One of the questions I asked every class at the end of the year was, "What did you like about the class, and what can I do to improve it?" Without fail, students appreciated the fact that I took their thoughts and feelings into account when making decisions. This is an easy thing to do, and it has a positive impact on the entire group.

Expect Them to Do What You Ask

The notion that singers flourish when they feel empowered does *not* mean that the director is disempowered. While you have more responsibilities than the singers, you have the same rights. This means that when you are running the rehearsal, you also have the right to be treated with respect. If you give the group a clear and direct instruction, do nothing else until they have met your expectations. *They will do what you expect them to do.* This may sound simple, but it is an area where so many of us are tempted to fudge a little, to the group's detriment.

Scenario: The singers are working with partners on a certain rhythmic challenge in a new piece of music. They are now ready to move to the next step in the learning process. You signal them to give you their support. Most of them are quietly looking at you, but there are a few who are still engaged in their own conversations. You think, "Should I wait until they are all looking at me. Well, we have a lot to do... and *most* of them are paying attention." *And you start to talk.* If you do this consistently, the group will learn very quickly that you don't mean what you say and your *actual* expectations of them are low. The environment in such a group will soon become unstable and unsafe.

Make Amends When Necessary

All of the above will help the group see you as supportive and trustworthy, but you cannot be an ideal human being all the time. We all make mistakes, sometimes choosing damaging words and actions that we later regret. When this happens, a simple and sincere apology can restore the safety and humanity of the group. For example:

> Folks, I blew it yesterday. I was in a lousy mood and brought my negative energy into the room. Stephanie took the brunt of it when I yelled at her for not memorizing her music. Stephanie, I am so sorry. Please accept this box of SweetTarts as a symbol of my sincere apology. (Done with sincerity, not with intent to bribe!)

I said words very similar to these to an eighth grade Drama class, and my doing so made all the difference. Stephanie was clearly grateful, while the rest of the class beamed huge smiles and expressed a collective, "Awww!" (That is "Awww" as in, "Isn't that sweet!" and not "Awww! Why does she get candy and we don't?") The atmosphere was cleared of tension, and we joyfully moved on with our rehearsal. Had I held on to my righteous pride, or not made amends for some other reason (embarrassment or fear of acknowledging my imperfection, perhaps), I would have lost their trust in me. And the safe atmosphere in the group would have been compromised. The good news is that you can always take responsibility and apologize, even if it's weeks after the incident. "Class, I did something three weeks ago that is still bothering me…" Fortunately, making amends does not have a statute of limitations.

Acknowledge your own humanness by taking responsibility for your actions. This rebuilds the group's sense of safety, and creates a powerful model of vulnerability and empathy for your students.

Director, Support Yourself

Conscious Awareness

It has helped me immeasurably to think of my career as a process of personal growth. When I began teaching and directing, I had a keen sense of fairness and sensitivity to others, but my ability to be fully confident and present needed lots of work. (I am pleased to report that I am still given opportunities for growth in this area!) But were my personal development not important to me, I would be much less evolved as a human being, and much less able to lead with confidence, authenticity, and sensitivity.

As I learned more in the personal growth arena, I hit upon a pivotal concept—Conscious Awareness. If you have conscious awareness, you are aware of your thoughts and feelings as they happen. Even better, you have the discernment to know which to act on, and which to set aside. In order to have a sensitive, confident, and expressive choir, it is extremely helpful for you as director to develop this moment-to-moment awareness. With it, you can consciously create that safe and supportive atmosphere. Without it, you can create just the opposite, and never know why.

A Director's Anger

Take a look at a director who gets angry, loses control, and yells at their singers. "Come on, people! That was awful! Sopranos, that was the ugliest tone I've heard in 15 years of teaching. If you don't care about the festival coming up, then I don't either. Why don't we all just stop trying?!" This may seem an extreme example, but I have seen even more "frustrated" outbursts.

What is going on here? This is a classic case of someone being unaware of their own inner process. A reactive and subconscious part of them was triggered and something snapped, creating an "overreaction." They "lost it." What specifically did they lose? They lost conscious awareness and the ability to make a supportive choice that was appropriate to the actual situation.

Many cases of frustration-related anger stem from feelings of inadequacy or worthlessness that we internalized many years ago. When this process occurs, the anger in the present moment acts as "protector," shielding us from those more painful feelings. The director above internalized the message that their value was tied to their accomplishments. So, when they started to "fail," they started to feel awful—worthless and small. Instead of feeling that pain, they got angry and felt BIG.

While not all cases of anger are frustration-related, most of them are tied to our pasts. We who lead others need to be particularly vigilant, especially when under stress—the temptation to give in to our angry impulses can be overwhelming. The fact that we are socially empowered as Leaders does not justify our acting out in anger, even though many people enable our doing so, excusing us as "temperamental artists." Their perception of us can change—so can we.

Clearly all of us are on different paths, carrying different types and amounts of emotional baggage. Regardless, going through life unaware of our issues will leave us at their mercy. We will feel their impact, and so will those around us. So will our choir.

Conscious Awareness In Action

Conscious awareness can help us understand ourselves, and it can help us better understand the singers in our choirs. The more we learn about what makes us act and react, the more we will learn about other people's behavior. This knowledge can help us interact with greater compassion, understanding, and sensitivity.

When a singer does something that gets under your skin...

1. Be aware that you are having a reaction. You might notice it as tightness in your body, a flush of negative emotion (fear, anger, entrapment, powerlessness), or a judgmental thought.

2. Assume responsibility for your reaction. Without expressing them, put your feelings "on ice." If possible, try to figure out what is causing this reaction. Look to your past—what does this feeling or situation remind you of? Be curious and open to your inner process.

3. Comfort yourself in the midst of your reaction. Apply compassion and understanding to the part of you that is having this reaction.

4. Be willing to see that the singer may be going through a similar experience—with something in *their* past (recent or otherwise) influencing *their* current behavior.

5. Let your conscious actions toward that singer be supportive, maintaining the safe atmosphere for everyone.

6. If you can't figure out where your reaction is coming from, keep working on it—it's bound to happen again.

If you keep your eyes and ears on your own reactions, they will be your teacher, guiding you to become a better director. When you stray from this path (and we all do), forgive yourself, make amends, and renew your commitment to the process.

Trouble with "Discipline"

We've looked at anger as a "red flag" that can lead us to awareness, personal growth, and more responsible behavior. Core feelings of worthlessness can also lead (more logically perhaps) to a lack of confidence or a sense of inadequacy. Often these feelings lead to ineffectual leadership. Do you feel that you are not in charge during the rehearsal?

- Do you want your singers to like you more than you want them to respect you? (Is your need to be liked greater than your desire to provide them with the absolute best musical experience?)
- Are you somehow uneasy, not trusting that everyone in the choir is paying attention?
- Do you continue to address the group, even though some people are talking or clearly not paying attention?
- Do you hold yourself back from insisting that people meet the highest standards of support?

- Do you have singers who "put down" other members of the choir while you ignore this behavior?
- Do you respond to such put-downs, but find that they continue?
- Do you justify the singers' lack of discipline and focus?
    They're young... They're seniors... It's early in the day... It's late... They're jocks... They're a community choir... They watch too much TV... Their lives are so stressful... They just don't get along with each other... They just like to have fun... They're emotionally immature... They're adolescent girls... They're boys—what do you expect?!

If you currently justify your choir's unsupportive behavior, you may be doing so to avoid facing some discomfort about yourself. Making the choir's lack of discipline "about them" is much easier than facing the part of you that is responsible. But you must face yourself if you want to create a safe place for your singers.

If you recognize yourself here, take heart in the fact that you are not alone. Many terrific people leading choirs of all sorts share your challenge. And your opportunity.

Practice Builds Confidence and Success

The feeling that you have neither the power nor the right to lead the group is uncomfortable, to say the least. I've been there, and for me it was terrifying. However, with patience, commitment, and conscious awareness you can turn the inward tide. But it takes practice. Put yourself right up against your edge—practice effective leadership as you would practice piano. Give yourself permission to expect the singers to meet the "highest and best" standards of behavior. But start slowly. Maybe the first time you'll only commit to expecting that they do what you ask for the first minute of class. The next day, stretch it to two minutes. Be prepared to squirm from discomfort while you are holding them to these uncompromising standards of behavior. In the midst of this process, you might feel passive and powerless, but there is strength in conviction! Do whatever it takes to get the complete support of every singer. Expect it. Calmly hold them to it. Accept nothing less. Gradually extend the time you are willing to require complete and total support until you are doing so for the entire rehearsal period.

A Safe Conclusion

In order to create Safety First in the choir, directors must have the highest expectations. They must expect the singers to treat each other with kindness, respect, and support. They must treat the singers with kindness, respect, and support. And perhaps most importantly, directors must treat themselves with kindness, respect, and support.

To create a safe choral environment is to embark on a most exciting journey, one that will bring unfathomable rewards to all involved. As the journey progresses, the singers will connect to the music with more passion, more commitment, and with much greater expression. Because it will be *safe* to do so.

2

Emotional Vulnerability

One's vulnerability allows another to experience a spirit and to engage a living soul through music. A more important component of an artistic relationship simply does not exist.

James Jordan, *The Musician's Soul*

I feel so open and vulnerable,
like I'm sharing who I really am for
the first time.

Workshop participant

The singer who felt "open and vulnerable" sang in a relatively safe choir. Singers in such groups are much more likely to risk emotional vulnerability (the open willingness to feel deeply and express those feelings completely). When singers are vulnerable, they and everyone around them, including the audience, experience their "naked truth." That truth is the stuff of great performances.

Just About Anybody Can Do It

It is certainly the case that some of us are more comfortable being vulnerable, and some of us less so. Some people are so confident and "out there" that they are able to express themselves honestly in any environment. But such people are extremely rare, and even they will be more expressive in an openly supportive environment.

Then there are those who find it difficult to share their feelings at all, especially when they sing. Some are shy, some are avoiding feeling, and some are defended, equating vulnerability with weakness. No matter the reason, most of us can grow to risk complete expression in a safe choir.

What's On Your Mind Is On Your Face

I often tell singers, "What's on your mind is on your face." If you are thinking of "vocal technique" or "getting the words right," that's what your face will express. If you are worried, your face will show it. If you are "playing it safe," resisting vulnerability by choosing to think and feel nothing, your face will show that. And for the audience, there is nothing less engaging than watching a singer's face express nothing!

There are singers who put on a generic "Happy Choral Face" when they sing, regardless of the text involved. Other singers look bored or depressed. Still others have "Intense Choral Face," always looking like they are worried about some dreadful event. Then there are those who manipulate their faces into what they believe will express the emotion or mood of the music. Even though this is not nearly enough to develop a complete and truthful connection, it does edge them slightly towards the goal. To understand why "putting on" an expression moves us closer to honest connection, let's take a look at emotional theory.

The Science of Emotion

The James/Lange Theory of Emotion, proposed in 1884, tells us that the body undergoes changes during certain perceived conditions. When these changes are experienced in the brain, they are experienced as emotion. For example, if we are hiking and see a rattlesnake on the path before us, we perceive that we are in "Danger!" Our bodies undergo a flush of adrenaline, and we freeze in our tracks. We then experience the emotion we call "fear."

While contemporary scientists are less inclined to agree that body changes come first and then create the emotion, there is still widespread agreement that there is a direct relationship between our emotions and our bodies, each affecting the other.

The brain is a phenomenally complicated mass of electricity, chemicals, neurons, synapses, and other organic matter. When a thought or feeling occurs, neurochemicals are released, millions of neurons fire electrical charges, signals are sent down the spinal column, and muscles are engaged throughout the body—especially on our faces. Spontaneous facial expressions occur as a result of that initial brain activity. Conversely, when we move the muscles on our faces, our brains associate the resulting expression with the corresponding neurochemical process. The associated neurons fire, electricity surges, the chemicals are released, and we experience feelings and thoughts that correspond to our facial expression. In other words, brain activity similar to that which *originates* a particular facial expression is also *activated by* that facial expression. According to Paul Newham, author of *Therapeutic Voicework: Principles and Practice for the Use of Singing as a Therapy*, a side benefit of encouraging this "outside in" exploration is that it can actually help singers discover unknown or dormant aspects of their personality.

Bottom line? Our emotions affect our facial expressions, and our facial expressions affect our emotions.

♦ An Exercise for You

If you want to experience the brain/body connection for yourself, furrow your brow and shout "NO!" repeatedly while **SLAMMING** a pillow against your bed. Shout "NO!" with every slam. Shout louder and louder, slam harder and harder. Commit yourself to this exploration. Even if you are feeling joyful and contented before you start, as you engage in the exercise you will notice yourself feeling some degree of anger or rage. You might even notice some thoughts starting to arise—thoughts that justify your anger!

♦ An Exercise for the Choir

For an easy and fun way to demonstrate this to singers, direct them as follows: Stand up. Slouch. Put on your best pout or frown. Whatever you do, DON'T SMILE. On my count, say, "I'm so excited!"

Stand tall, shoulders back (but not forced), hips tucked under, feet shoulder width apart. Lift those eyebrows and cheekbones and SMILE. Say, "I'm so depressed!"

OK. This time, slouch. Pout or frown. DON'T SMILE. Now say, "I'm so depressed!"

Now stand tall, shoulders back, hips tucked under, feet shoulder width apart. SMILE. Say, "I'm so excited!"

"What did you notice?"

Have the singers process their experience briefly with their neighbors. When those feeling safe enough to share with the group do so, you will hear comments like, "It felt weird to smile and say, 'I'm so depressed.' I just didn't believe myself." "My voice sounded different when I was saying what I was really feeling. When I was lying my voice didn't have the same conviction." And, "It just felt more *right* to have the body, words, and emotions 'match up.'"

They will most likely agree that their facial expressions and body alignment have an undeniable effect on the way that they feel, and on the ability to feel truthfully connected to emotion.

Jump-Start the Emotion

Once we understand the science of emotion, the benefit of singers "putting on" a certain facial expression becomes clear. When they shift their face to an expression that the mind associates with anger (furrowed brow, narrowed eyes), they are likely to start *feeling angry*. When they lift their cheekbones, and raise their upper lip and eyebrows, they are likely to feel emotions akin to joy. For this reason, it can be helpful to invite singers to use this technique to jump-start their own emotions. They can then build on these feelings to complete their truthful connection as they continue to sing. This way, even though they start with a little "trickery," they can use it to help them connect to their complete truth.

Scenario: The singers are having a terrible day—everything that could go wrong has gone wrong; they are *down*. To add to the misery, it's raining and the roof is leaking. And now they have to sing Lloyd Pfautsch's *i thank you God* (an amazingly joyous piece of music with text by ee cummings).

You can help them reconnect to joy and appreciation by suggesting they jump-start their connection with a smile.

The Truth Lies In Our Faces

This jump-starting works to an extent, but it can only begin the process of genuine connection. It is much too general, and as such, will not lead us to specific thoughts and feelings that motivate a compelling moment-to-moment musical experience. And while it is better than having no emotional vulnerability at all, it will not fool the audience.

Even if we try to fake it for their benefit, the audience is comprised of people who, as social beings, have learned to read faces. They have the skills to recognize the slightest non-verbal signals that communicate sincerity or falsehood. The smallest muscular contraction on the sides of the eyes, for example, accompanies a genuine smile. Most people couldn't tell you that they know this, but they know it, nonetheless. And because they know it, and other subtle visual cues, they are able to discern whether our joy is actual or simulated, total or incomplete, general or specific.

> The audience knows when we are truthfully connecting to the words and the music, and they know when we are faking it.

The Audience Reads Voices, Too

From early infancy we begin to make sense not only of our fellow humans' faces, but their tone of voice as well. Paul Ekman, the author of *Emotions Revealed*, sees the face and voice as "a dual system" of expression. He spent eight years of research codifying ten thousand different facial muscle combinations and their emotional meanings (resulting in the Facial Action Coding System, or FACS). And while he hasn't studied the voice as extensively, he is aware of its direct relationship to emotion. According to Ekman, when it comes to understanding the subtleties of expression, "The voice is every bit as important as the face."

Connecting to Meaning

Even the child at 12 months is aware of subtle shifts of meaning when the speaker's tone changes. As we grow older, we get more and more sophisticated in our awareness of human communication subtleties. It makes sense, then, that our discernment of the human voice extends to singing, arguably the most "human" of all the musical arts when it is connected directly to the psyche. In Meredith Willson's classic musical, *The Music Man*, Harold Hill says, "Singing is only sustained talking." And while some voice teachers might disagree with Professor Hill's statement, few neuroscientists would dispute it—virtually identical neurochemical processes occur in both speaking and singing, and with the same results—assuming that both the speaker and singer are equally connected. All this leads us to the following fact: Singing carries meaning just as speaking does. And the audience, having honed their skills since toddlerhood, can detect when that meaning is there, and when it is lacking.

This may seem obvious. After all, legendary singers like Ray Charles, Billie Holiday, and Barbra Streisand are icons the world over because of their ability to communicate human meaning through song. Even a populist like Barry Manilow owes much of his success to truthful and meaningful expression. When *Oprah* staff members asked one audience member why she liked Barry Manilow so much, the woman gasped, "Have you ever *watched* the way he *sings*?!"

For further evidence of the power of meaningful singing, look at all the people who have been moved to tears during powerful musical theatre or opera performances. Observe the effect that singers like Cecilia Bartoli, Bryn Terfel, or Frederica von Stade have on their audiences. Maria Callas, the great operatic soprano, was famous the world over for her charismatic presence. Why? Because her singing was an expression of her being that connected her to her characters, her music, and her audience. Her primary artistic goal was to sing with expression, with feeling—to make sure that her words and musical expression had meaning. Her audiences were captivated. Singing can carry great meaning, and when it does, we are affected deeply.

The flip side of this is also true. When a singer communicates less meaning, we are affected less deeply. The following review of a major operatic star illustrates this truth. As Joshua Kosman (San Francisco Chronicle music critic) writes:

> [The singer] sounded almost unnervingly great... But with the possible exception of her final death scene, [the singer] never seemed to connect those musical phrases with the emotional torment of a real person. As she went through the motions faithfully, there was an inevitable blankness lurking just behind the notes.

Another reviewer, Tim Ashley of the Guardian Unlimited (London) says of the same singer:

> All too often we're asked to admire technique rather than musical meaning.

♦ An Exercise for the Choir

Invite the singers to work in pairs, each person thinking of a fun, exciting, or humorous experience they would feel comfortable sharing. Each person is designated A or B. On your count of "1, 2, 3, Go!" the A's talk, trying to get the B's enthused while the B's listen and watch A's face. After about 5 seconds, shout "Switch" (or use some other signal) at which time the A's SING as they continue the story. After another 5 seconds or so, shout "Switch" again and the A's stop singing and continue the story through speech. After 5 seconds, they "Switch" again, continuing with song. Do this for about one minute, then it's the B's turn to share their experience while the A's watch and listen. Repeat the "Switch" process for another minute or so before you stop and discuss.

About the Exercise

- This is a "scary" exercise so it really helps if you do a demonstration first, with one of them giving you the countdown and telling you when to switch.
- The exercise works well when done early on in the group's process, but can also be helpful when you are discussing Imagery (Chapter 6).

Questions for the Group

- How many of you noticed that your partner's face was expressive, going through lots of changes as they told the story?
- Did their face continue to be expressive when they sang?
- How many of you had pictures or mental movies going through your head as you were telling the story? How about when you were listening to the story?
- How many of you had specific thoughts and feelings as you were telling the story? As you were listening?

After their feedback, tell them that this is another example of the adage, "What's on your mind is on your face." Singing can be just as expressive as speaking if specific thoughts and feelings are connecting us to the words and music we sing. To whet their appetite for the opportunities ahead, I tell them something like this:

> If you chose to sing your partner's "song," you could interview them, getting lots of details so your thoughts and feelings would be as rich as theirs. (What were you thinking and feeling when your parachute wouldn't open? How high were you? What did you see when you looked down? Was the lake clear, turquoise, muddy, or deep blue? What was the weather like? What was your suit like?) When you sing most songs, however, you don't have the luxury of being able to quiz the composer or the poet who wrote the words. What you do have is the opportunity to create all those specific details using your imagination. And the great thing is, *the brain doesn't know the difference between what you imagine and what is real,* so you can be just as engaged with "someone else's" words and stories—if you make them your own.

The Composer Can't Do It for Us

While this concept may seem like a no-brainer, we choristers often make the mistake of assuming that singing *automatically* incorporates meaning. After all, the composers, if they are any good, build meaning into the music with melody, rhythm, harmony, dissonance, and chord progression, right? Well, sort of, but not really. This is no truer than saying that playwrights build meaning into the actors' lines through word choice, rhythm, setting, plot, characterization, and conflict.

The truth is that composers help us with all of their structures, but their ability to guide us ends at the printed page. If the singers fail to connect truthfully and meaningfully to the music, the composer's meaning won't make it to the audience in as powerful and poignant a way as it would otherwise. In such a scenario, a magnificent sounding choir may be IMpressive, but it won't be EXpressive.

The House of Connection

Even though composers do a considerable amount, they are limited. They are like architects who draw up the most detailed blueprints, but must then rely on the skill and dedication of others to realize their vision. In the choral music world, the composer creates the musical "blueprint," but must rely on us to complete the project. With the director as "contractor," individual singers lay the foundation, build the frame, plumb and wire, paint, furnish, and decorate. By this end of the process, each singer has fleshed out the composer's vision. The House of Connection is built, vital and breathing.

If we don't humanize the composer's blueprint, the final product will be "just another pretty song" devoid of warmth or depth—technically perfect, perhaps, but sterile and uninviting. "A hymn is not a hymn sung with no heart" growls new folk artist Greg Brown in his song, *My New Book*. As most any composer will concur, a song carries heart or human meaning only when the singer puts it there. This is what we as choral artists need to deeply understand. We must "put it there" if we want our humanness to be expressed in the music, since it doesn't get there through the will of the composer, by itself, or through any other means. Why is this so important? Because the audience can tell when we are communicating genuine human meaning, and when we are merely singing words, pitches, and rhythms. They know not only by our faces, but also by the sound of our voices.

◆ An Exercise for You or the Choir

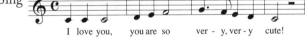

Sing

I love you,   you are so   ver - y, ver - y cute!

The first time, try to sing with flawless vocal technique. Concentrate on diction, breath, open vowels, line, resonance, and beautiful tone, all this while looking at a wall. Notice how you sound, and how you feel. Record yourself, if you like, or work with a partner with whom you can exchange feedback.

The second time, sing—or imagine you're singing—to a loved one. (This could be a child of yours, a pet, or a significant other.) This time, concentrate hard and sing with the same vocal "excellence" while looking at the loved one. Notice how you sound, and how you feel.

The third time, think about all the things you love about this wonderful individual, and what *specifically* makes them so special. When you are connected to these thoughts and feelings, sing to them again, but this time concentrate on letting them know just how much you love and adore them. Make sure they "get it." Notice how you sound, and how you feel.

The fourth time, use your imagination (or draw from real life) and come up with a reason to be angry towards this individual. Maybe they spilled something on your newly cleaned carpet. Maybe they shared a personal quirk of yours at your boss's dinner party. If they're a pet, maybe they "had an accident." Who knows?! Just make sure you know exactly what they did and how you feel about it. Now, try and make them cringe from guilt and feel terrible when you sing those (now sarcastic) words to them. Notice how you sound, and how you feel.

What did you notice after all that? Chances are you felt the most connected to your genuine human experience of love and adoration during your third rendition of the song. Did you? If not, sing it again and try to get the individual to smile (or wag their tail!) as you are "gushing" love at them. Chances are also good that your sound was more nuanced on the third and fourth go-round. Ask your partner and/or your loved one to tell you what they heard during your four different versions. The differences may have been either blatant or subtle, but they were very likely present.

The Impact of Connection

Truthful Connection Affects Sound

Our emotional connection affects our facial expression, and our facial expression affects our sound.

When singing the above song and connecting to your own feelings, your face spontaneously changed. (Remember those brain signals?) Your loving connection might have brought a slight smile to your face, lifted your cheeks, or raised your eyebrows. Your sarcastic "guilt attack" might have furrowed your brow, narrowed your eyes, or contracted your cheek muscles. All of these facial changes affect the shape of the resonance chamber that includes your mouth, sinuses, and throat, leading to subtle shifts in vowel sound and resonance. Thus, when singers' faces are engaged with their emotions, their voices are more expressive. They are able to communicate more nuance and tonal color. When the singers' collective truth connects to the truth of the music, the choir naturally sounds different, and the audience hears and understands the meaning of this difference.

Royal Stanton, in his book, *Steps to Singing for Voice Classes*, calls this type of singing "artistic," and likens the voice of the expressive singer to freshly brewed coffee.

> Artistic singing always sounds new, fresh, and vital. What is the difference between the smell of the coffee while it is being brewed and its fragrance two hours later? When it is being reheated, it is still coffee—same liquid, same color—but its most pleasing aspect has flown away. Similarly, the artistic performance never sounds "warmed over." The artistry consists in making the music sound "freshly brewed," as though the performer were creating it right on the spot for the first and only time. This lends it excitement, vitality, and a fleeting quality of newness that, like the smell of coffee, is unique.

Face, Voice, and Body

The face and the voice are not the only things affected by the connected brain's outgoing signals. The rest of the body is also impacted, including the muscles involved with the breath. When you were singing of love and cuteness, your breath may have been "caressing" the words, resulting in a gentle legato phrase. When attacking and guilting, your consonants might have been more punched, your breath energy and volume higher. You might have sung some words with strong *staccato* or *marcato* accents. Regardless of the emotional subtlety, most singers experience a much more direct connection to the breath when they are also connected to the truth.

When the emotional connection is extreme anger, the heightened breath energy will affect volume for sure. If the composer and director are calling for the anger to be expressed *piano* or *pianissimo* rather than *fortissimo*, the heightened breath energy will affect vocal intensity. When a singer's facial and breath energy is aligned with anger, the consonants will be more "punched." Actually, *any* truthful connection will affect tonal quality, whether the connection elicits the utmost tenderness, the most violent rage, or anything in between.

Let's say the line of text is, "Throw your cursed weapons down!" And the song is a powerful anti-war anthem, written after the composer lost her son in what she viewed as a pointless "military action." If each singer in the group connects personally and powerfully to the anger behind the line, the audience will get it. There will be no doubt. "What a sweet love song" will NOT be a comment whispered ear to ear during the applause. If the audience members' eyes were closed, they would still accurately interpret the singers' emotional connection. You might have had the experience of listening to a choir sing in an unknown language, but still understanding their emotions. Those singers were probably deeply connected to meaning.

Just as the audience hears the singers' meaning, so do they see subtleties of expression in the singers' bodies. There are subtle differences in posture and muscular/skeletal orientation depending on the singers' exact connection, and if movement is involved, the moves will "come alive" if the singers are "putting" their connection and feeling into the music. Even something as simple as hand clapping can be infused with purpose, passion, and power if the singer truthfully connects. I'm sure you've seen the difference between passionately joyful clapping and timid, uncommitted, or disconnected clapping. What a difference for the singers and the audience when the singers really "get into it"!

Emphasis and Figurative Language

It's amazing how many nuances of meaning there are when we connect!
Workshop participant

When we are emotionally vulnerable enough to truthfully connect to text and meaning, the brain and body work together to naturally emphasize appropriate words. Whether our words are literal or figurative, the emphasis will communicate appropriate meaning. "You are so *cute!*" we might sing. Or "I *love* you." Composers try to lead us to this meaningful interpretation through rhythm, note duration, dynamic markings, or lyric placement on a particular note. But these are only *external* cues. When we understand the inherent meaning and *communicate that meaning* as we sing, we add the human dimension. We finish "the building." And the meaning reaches way past the page and into the audience. They get it.

> The audience pays attention to singers' faces, bodies, and voices to find out what the music means, and how the singers feel about it. If the audience only wants to know what the choir is singing, they can read the text.

Along with emphasis comes Subtext, the *real* meaning "beneath" certain words and phrases. When you sang "I love you, you are so very, very cute!" while guilting your loved one, the words did not match your meaning. Your actual meaning may have been, "I hate it when you put me down in front of company! I don't appreciate it at all!"

If the faces, bodies, and voices don't match either the figurative or literal meaning of the words, the audience will notice this incongruence, and it will prevent them from fully engaging with the choir. If the singers connect to the intended meaning, and actively communicate that connection, the audience will get that meaning in triplicate—face, voice, and body.

The Magic Between Choir and Audience

If you had asked your loved one or partner what they experienced during your "I love you" exercise, they might have told you of a "magical" happening. Scientists who study emotion and the brain have discovered some amazing things about what happens to us when we watch another human being express their feelings.

One of the most powerful findings is that we humans automatically mimic certain facial expressions when we see them on other people. Babies mimic their caretakers' expressions almost from day one of their existence. As we get older, our ability to mimic becomes more sophisticated, in parallel with our ability to read faces. Think of all the times during the day when you pass by someone you don't know, whether on the street, in the hall, or at the grocery store. Even though you don't know them, they smile at you and you smile back. This reflex is especially powerful with smiling, but is present during many other expressions. Think of what happens to you when you are watching a gripping movie (or reality show!), and one of the characters starts "the crying process." If they are connected, their face will present an accurate reflection of their feelings, and you might start to feel similar emotions. For me, my breath gets shallow, I feel a tightness in my chest, my face contracts, and tears leak down my cheeks. This happens, by the way, even if I turn the television on and catch that moment and that moment only. If you've ever been to a funeral and watched a speaker become overwhelmed by emotion, you may have experienced something similar. Scientific term? "Physiological synchrony." (For more information, read *Empathic Accuracy* by William Ickes, editor, and *Bodymind & Voice, Book One* by Thurman.)

Physiological synchrony is impactful in and of itself, but when combined with certain other processes, its effect intensifies. As you already know, if you smile for whatever reason, you are going to start feeling emotion related to smiling due to the neurochemicals that will be released in the brain. Here's where the magic starts to really take hold.

Scenario: The choir is singing a fabulous, dynamic, and upbeat spiritual. The audience members pan the group, and wherever they look they see singers smiling a genuine and connected smile. What happens? The audience members smile "back" as a reflex, then start to feel joy. The more connected the singers are, the more their faces will show it. The more the singers' faces are expressing, the more the audiences will feel emotions akin to that expression. Scientific term? "Emotional synchrony."

When this process occurs, the audience members get an "emotional boost" from the fact that they are smiling. As they continue to look at different singers, they see *more* smiling which they then "return," thus releasing more neurochemicals and causing them to smile even more. If they notice they're having a great time and think, "This is a blast!" even more neurochemicals are released. This can lead to some serious delirium on the part of the audience members, as anyone who has experienced this phenomena will attest. After attending such a concert, one might say, "I was smiling so much it hurt!"

Social anthropologists theorize that physiological and emotional synchrony may have helped early societies of humans bond, develop empathy, function as a cohesive unit, and ultimately survive. But whatever the early function of our species' "magical" abilities, the result is undeniable. We mimic each other, passing the "baton of feelings" as we do so.

But the magic doesn't stop with mimicry and its associated brain activity. If we combine the principles of physiological synchrony, emotional synchrony, and our ability to "read" each other's feelings (via their faces, voices, and bodies), we realize that humans naturally have the capacity to feel what others around them are feeling. As Steven Johnson writes in *Mind Wide Open: Your Brain and the Neuroscience of Everyday Life*:

> It turns out that one of the brain's greatest evolutionary achievements is its ability to model the mental events occurring in other brains.

Johnson discusses a related "trick" of the mind. Scientists in the late 1990's discovered "mirror neurons" that fire in the brains of monkeys both when a monkey does a certain task, and when a monkey sees another monkey do that same task. This suggests "that the brain is designed to draw analogies between our own mental and physical states and those of other individuals."

And there is still one more rabbit to be pulled out of the hat. When we observe people feeling something, we don't always feel the same emotion that they're experiencing. But the very fact that they are feeling stimulates us to feel something as well. Take the example of watching someone who is in anguish. While we sometimes go into anguish ourselves, we often feel something like pity, sympathy, sadness, or concern. However, our specific response is not what's important here. What is important is that the more extreme the emotional expression of the person being watched, the more extreme our emotional response. Think about the difference between seeing someone at work brush away a few tears (after hearing the news that they didn't get a raise), and seeing someone distraught and hysterical (after learning that their spouse was just killed in an accident). Their two responses are dramatically different, and so would be our own likely emotional responses as we observed them—even if we didn't know the cause of either person's upset.

This has clear relevance for all involved with choral music. When audiences experience a truthfully connected and expressive choir, they have a corresponding emotional response. Whether they feel something similar to what the choir is feeling, or they experience another feeling stimulated by the singers' expression, the important thing is that they are feeling. So, *if* we want to consistently and powerfully engage the audience on an emotional level, the singers *must* be connected to the music.

The power of this experience for audience members cannot be overstated. It helps them to connect to their own emotions, and reinvigorates their senses of empathy, bonding, and community. They experience a level of feeling and connectedness with themselves and others that they might miss in their daily lives. When they attend an expressive choir's concert, they are in for a treat. The choir's gift of expression can help the audience members connect to their own sense of what it means to be human.

The Singers and Connection

The Joy of Connected Singing

At almost every workshop I have led, one person has volunteered that singing with this newfound vulnerability and connection is "easier and more fun." As they explain, it's easier because they now have an internally motivated reason for singing that gives them an exciting sense of purpose. This gives their singing an energy that it had previously lacked, and the song almost "sings itself."

As for "more fun," the singers explain that they now are thinking and feeling "all sorts of cool things." They also feel empowered, like they have become part of the creative process, not just a "key on a 'choral piano' played by the director." Using truthful connection, the choral experience becomes more than the quest for the best choral sound, or the group's best possible performance of a particular song. Once singers are vulnerable and willing to risk, the choir can become a medium for powerful personal and group expression.

Because each singer commits to the process, the energy bounces around the entire group, invigorating everyone and adding to the sense of "fun" and "ease of singing." As one workshop participant said, "I really felt the energy of the group, and it inspired me." Commitment is infectious.

This "fun" and connected singing has one significant benefit—it relaxes the singing mechanism. When singers are concentrating on technical elements of singing, they often create tension in their bodies—in the tongue and jaw especially. When the singing comes "from the heart," this unnecessary tension dissipates. Ultimately, it becomes easier to sing without tension, and easier to sustain strong singing throughout an entire concert.

Each Singer's Awesome Responsibility

The good news is that expressive singing is fun and rewarding—singers will quickly embrace it. However, some singers may need a little extra motivation to realize how important their individual expression actually is. Often, these are the same singers that feel they can remain anonymous since they are in a choir. Nothing could be further from the truth; each singer needs to think of themselves as the only person singing.

To impress upon singers their awesome responsibility, I tell them that chances are good that at least one audience member is watching them at any given moment during a concert. Since they have no way of knowing when they're being watched and when they're not, they have to assume that they're being watched constantly. When an audience member looks at an unexpressive singer, that magic moment of connection is lost for both.

This concept can help motivate singers who hold back from expressing because they are afraid of "standing out." When the audience pans the group, the singer doing something different will catch their attention. So, if the whole group is connecting except for one singer, that one singer will get more than their fair share of notice! One director I know uses this point to great effect with his elementary school singers.

The fact that the audience watches everyone and focuses on those who are different means that each singer is responsible for connection and expression all the time, each and every moment. This is a solemn yet invigorating obligation that comes with a gigantic payoff: When you connect with yourself, you connect with the audience.

*I would prefer to give them a copy of the text w/out the music & prior to singing or even listening to the music. Read it several times as a poem or narrative. Possibly answering questi... put before them by the director.

38

Dealing with Emotional Overwhelm

Occasionally, truthfully connecting to the music will bring up overwhelming emotions in a singer. These emotions can lead to tears and other physical manifestations that can make it difficult or impossible to sing. However, if the singers rehearse with full connection, they will almost always be able to fine-tune it—learning how much is too much, how personal is too personal. They will then be able to perform with expression without being surprised by "too much" emotion.

If singers do become overwhelmed during performance, there are things they can do to stabilize. If singers worked with these feelings during rehearsals, they will likely have the wherewithal to lower the intensity of their connection, while still maintaining it overall. Another option is for them to temporarily disconnect from meaning and focus entirely on the technical aspects of singing. Breathing deeply while relaxing the throat and the chest will help as well.

The Director and Connection

The words and music made sense to me for the first time.
Workshop participant (singer)

When Singers Do More

Ironically, though truthful expression begins with each individual singer, the whole choir benefits. So does the director.

Remember the composer whose artistic vision the choir is trying to communicate? The composer's creative source of expression is human experience—they experience the world through their human brain and heart, and put their thoughts and feelings into their music. But human experience is something that we all share, so each of us is familiar with the composer's source to some extent. We've either experienced similar events and feelings, or we can imagine them. So, when the singers tap into their *own* human experience as it relates to the music, they are tapping into the composer's source as well. By doing so, they have advanced their understanding of the music because they have found a way to relate to it *at its source*. Hence the statement, "The words and music made sense to me for the first time."

When every singer taps into the common source that inspired the music, it has an impact on the whole choir—their singing is more unified. They are actually connecting to each other via the same source. With such a choir, the director conducts a living expression of connected thought and feeling, and needs to do much less work to unify the sound. The singers are already there.

Working with a small adult choir, I was struck by the truth of all this. Before the group worked on each individual song, they sounded a tad "sloppy" and disunified, like a bunch of soloists trying in vain to understand the choral singing concept. Then the singers applied the truthful connection process and sang the song again. With each of their seven pieces, the difference was striking. When they connected to the composer's music via the shared source of human experience, their singing was much more cohesive. Their phrasing was together, their cutoffs were crisp, their vowels were unified, their dynamics were in sync. It was as if they had moved ahead about a month in a typical rehearsal process. With such a group, the director can start from a place very close to the composer's source, and then work to connect the choir even more specifically and powerfully to the music. After her choir used just one truthful connection technique, Karen Silva (a California Music Educators Association representative) wrote in a CMEA newsletter, "It was amazing how much more musical the piece had become..."

When all singers connect to their own human source, they bring wonderful gifts to the director. The director experiences new levels, new meanings, new subtleties, new energy, new sounds, and new excitement. This is similar to any human collaborative endeavor—when each individual connects to the shared goal with passion and purpose, every member of the team is inspired, including the leader.

This has strong parallels in the theatre world in which some directors guide actors in a process that connects them deeply and truthfully to the world of the play, while others treat actors like puppets, controlling their every moment on stage. ("Before your line, raise your eyebrows, look confused, wait three seconds, then turn upstage and deliver the line like this.") Actors generally much prefer working with the former director, because the actor's stage experience can then be imbued with truth, spontaneity, creativity, passion, and true "in-the-moment" presence. In short, the actors connect to all that is authentically human, and are given the responsibility and re-spect that they, as collaborative artists, deserve. The reward for the actors is huge since they get to feel the electric vibrancy of real life as they connect themselves to their characters. Of course, rewards are there in abundance for the audience as well. Chances are good that if you saw two plays, one "human-directed" and one "puppeted," you would probably be much more affected by the former, even though you might not know why. So it is with choral performances.

The Director Can Relax

So many times I've looked at my choir and thought that there must be a magic key someplace to unlock this paralysis of spirit.

James Jordan, *The Musician's Soul*, 1999

How many times have you watched a director go through all sorts of facial gymnastics while their bodies gyrated, implored, demanded, twitched, self-combusted… ANYTHING to get those singers to be expressive! It's a cruel amusement to watch this futile tug-of-war, because the director's energy far exceeds the combined expressive energy of the choir (or so it seems!). The director, who is working so furiously to accomplish so little, "wins" the Battle of Energy, and loses the War of Expression.

Scenario: The choir just sang its first song and the audience cheers wildly. The singers beam their appreciation, sending the thought, "Thank you, I'm so glad you liked that! I enjoyed singing it for you." As the applause settles, the director places a hand over his or her own heart. This is the signal for the singers to establish their truthful connection before the downbeat, and a very important signal it is.

> When the choir is connecting, I don't feel responsible for their connection anymore. I can relax and enjoy the process of making music.
>
> A high school director during a workshop

When a director can let go of that responsibility, entrusting and empowering each singer to take it on instead, the director can focus on other things. Things like making music, as the director quoted above attests. During performance, if the director notices that the singers have lost their connection, all the director need do is give them a signal (a pointing to the heart or the head, for instance). This is so much easier than contorting the face into a "violent mask of expression," hoping that at least a couple of singers will respond!

Learning the Music

Of course, the singers will have the greatest potential for expression if they learn their music and sing without scores. To do this most efficiently, Leon Thurman advocates separating rhythms and pitches from text, singing them first on a neutral syllable. Once the singers have done this a few times, have them "add" the words, following along with their fingers (thus incorporating more of the brain). Then, "Close the music. Let's see how we do." Thurman encourages similar approaches throughout the music-making process, always stressing the pursuit of shared goals and "innacuracy-free learning" rather than the consistent and relentless focusing on a singer's "mistakes."

The Way You Rehearse Is the Way They Perform

I can't tell you the e-mails that I receive... asking how I get my choristers to be so involved with the music. The answer? We work on this as hard as we work on the music. Tenacity is the key factor. It can't be said occasionally. It has to be part of each and every rehearsal.

Mary Alice Stollak, director of the Michigan State University Children's Chorus

In order for you to make the most of the choir's potential, it is vital that you incorporate truthful connection principles from day one, and apply them on a consistent and regular basis. The singers need to get used to being emotionally vulnerable, they need to build trust, they need to risk, and they need to prepare their connections specifically and methodically. You also need to work with the changes (emotional, physical, and tonal) that the singers will bring to the rehearsal as a result of their connection. This is very doable, however, and will only make the rehearsals better, bringing more depth to the music, and bringing it earlier. Waiting until right before the concert to "add expression" is much less effective.

You cannot make perfection the goal and then later decide you are going to 'add' emotion or say something personal about the words. Emotion/expression changes the voice and the body, and that is why it needs to develop in tandem with technical development.

Cynthia Hoffman, Master Teacher, from A Spectrum of Voices by Elizabeth Blades-Zeller

In Bodymind and Voice, Book One, Thurman addresses this issue, bringing an amazing degree of scientific evidence to bear on the discussion. I highly recommend Book One in particular for a comprehensive look at the science behind human expression, supportive directing, and what Thurman calls "human-compatible learning." (When I read it I was stunned to see my own thoughts and philosophies so laid out, analyzed, and substantiated.)

One of Thurman's points is that the singers will learn the music faster when they engage their own humanity and imagination. Why? In a nutshell, more neural pathways are built in the brain. The scientific formula might look like this:

> Imagination
> + Memories
> + Feelings
> + Text
> + Music = GREATER BRAIN INVOLVEMENT

Since neurons are numbered in the billions and synapses in the hundreds of trillions, singers now have many more ways to access the stored information, and it becomes easier, quicker, and more fulfilling to learn.

The Comfortable Choir

When we are *self*-conscious, we cannot be wholly aware; we must throw ourselves out first. This throwing ourselves away is the act of creativity.
Madeline L'Engle, *A Circle of Quiet* (1972)

Another benefit is that the more you rehearse with the truthful connection principles, the more comfortable and relaxed the singers will be in performance. Since they created and strengthened their brain's complex neural pathways during rehearsal, they can now focus on their "inner life" which will sustain their connection during performance. Because of this, *self*-consciousness—one of the factors preventing a charismatic performance—will be lessened dramatically. Stage fright can become a thing of the past.

If you're concerned that I'm suggesting you work on connection and expression every minute of every rehearsal, fear not. Rehearsals require you to focus on different elements at different times, and it's sometimes necessary to work on notes the entire rehearsal. However, even in such situations—when your focus is on technical elements—the singers can still weave connection into the tapestry. Whether they do it alone, or you lead them in it, incorporating the two areas in each rehearsal can be done seamlessly, making both the technical and the expressive elements richer for their collaboration.

Inhibitions

In order for the above to work, you need to have laid the groundwork, doing your best to create that safe and supportive environment where emotional vulnerability is not only possible but exciting. However, even after creating a nurturing environment, you will probably still have certain challenges.

- You may need to help inhibited singers become less so.

- You may need to "rehumanize" singers who have been trained to sing "perfectly" while disconnecting from their emotions.

- You may need to help singers actually become aware of and use facial expression.

- You may need to help singers identify when they are connecting truthfully, and when they are "faking it."

The exercises in Appendix One—though in the back of the book—are *integral*. They will help singers connect and express with passion and confidence.

The Inner Critic   *good!*

One of the strongest forces that inhibit us and work against expression is the Inner Critic. Everyone has this internal judge—the part of us that finds fault with our own words, actions, thoughts, and feelings—but some of us have found a way to quiet the mental condemnation to a tolerable level. Many of us, however, are not so fortunate; our inner critic speaks so loudly and so often that our expressive self cowers in the shadows.

> "You look weird doing that!" the inner critic might yell when we try a particular exercise... *And we suppress our commitment to the exercise.*
>
> "People can hear you and your voice might crack!" the inner critic might shout as we try a connected *fortissimo... And our voice withers.*
>
> "People will think you look like a dork!" The inner critic might roar as we find our faces reacting naturally to a strong feeling as we sing... *And our face retreats into blank nothingness.*

As this cerebral judge is really a well-meaning attempt at self-protection, I suggest to my students that they address their inner critic, saying something like, "Thanks for being here, buddy. I really appreciate it. But I can do this without you, and I need you to back off if I'm going to be fully expressive!" This works for many people, as does telling that part of themselves that, "Everyone else is going for it, so what's the big deal?!"

Help the singers become aware of their inner critic and give them the tools they need to overcome its crippling influence. Creating a safe atmosphere will help, but many individuals will still be negatively impacted by it regardless of the group's support. Luckily, there's more you can do.

The Inner Critic Questions   *good!*

Here are some questions to ask whenever you sense the group is suffering from overactive "Coolness Cops" (a synonym that resonates especially well with younger singers).

- How many of you were aware of your inner critic?
- What was your inner critic telling you?
- How did the inner critic affect your voice? Body? Mind?
- Did anybody find a way to deal with your inner critic and commit more completely?
- Was anybody's inner critic just too strong to overcome that time? Why do you think that is?
- What is it like to express yourself with a smaller, or even an absent, inner critic?

After challenging the group to deal with the inner critic, you might say, "Did you happen to notice if your inner critic was quieter this time?"

I have used the inner critic questions with literally thousands of students over the years and am convinced: A person will become more confident and more expressive through awareness and discussion of the inner critic. As with all personal growth, awareness must come first. Only after the singer develops awareness can they take steps to free themselves from the inner critic's stifling impact. With your guidance, their singing will become more expressive as they learn to "know their enemy." Once the inner critic is held up to the light of awareness, its power will fade.

Acknowledging their own inner critic in a public forum can help release the singers from its power. "My name is Tom Carter and I have an inner critic" can be freeing in and of itself, just like acknowledging ones addiction in a program like Alcoholics Anonymous. As in those support groups, hearing how others are affected by and have learned to cope with their inner critic can be most helpful. The singer is no longer alone with their "shameful secret"—they now know it's just a part of the human condition. Most significantly in the choral context, it is now possible for the singer to overcome the inner critic's effect and become a fully expressive artist.

Perfectionism and the Inner Critic

When the director strives for musical "perfection" without giving an equal amount of weight to the humanity underneath, the singers will never be fully expressive. Such a directorial approach stifles most singers' authenticity—they are so concerned with being "perfect" that they don't feel free to risk being human. In such a choir, the singers' inner critic is on constant alert.

Since striving for perfection is one way many directors try to keep their own inner critic at bay, the following quote by composer Ned Rorem might prove a useful reflection.

> Perfection is no more a requisite to art than to heroes. Frigidaires are perfect. Beauty limps. My frigidaire has had to be replaced.
>
> Ned Rorem, "Random Notes from a Diary," *Music From Inside Out*

The ongoing relationship between musical perfection and the benefits of vulnerability is wonderfully described by an American choral icon. In *The Robert Shaw Reader* (Yale University Press, 2004), editor Robert Blocker includes Shaw's notes to the choir. Writing about Barber and Neruda's process of sharing their individual souls in the music and text of *The Lovers*, Shaw writes:

> The corollary for the performer is that precisely at the point at which one touches his "deepest," and most vulnerable, unsharable selfawareness he touches all other men.
>
> R
>
> P.S. Now, learn your notes.

3

Truth, Tone, & Technique

What comes from the mouth goes to the ear,
but what comes from the heart goes to the heart.
Ancient Hindu proverb

Our director doesn't want us to smile.
Workshop participant

I imagine there might be some readers who think, "What about choral tone? Won't the sound suffer since vowels and resonance will be affected by the singers' facial expressions? Isn't this reason enough to dismiss the "truthful connection" process?" While connecting to the source will help to unify and humanize the voices, some readers may still be concerned with its impact on the beauty of the sound. This fear is understandable, but entirely unnecessary. Truthfully expressive choirs have wowed the audiences at national music conventions and concerts, and won prestigious international choral festivals. Truthful expression does not create ugly sound. Not even close. If the appropriate vocal technique is combined with authentic connection, the choral sound will be no less beautiful, and much more dynamic and engaging. Dr. Charlene Archibeque commented after a coaching session with the San José State University Choraliers, "I was truly amazed at the change in involvement and sound."

Frowning at the Inner Smile

Let's look at one fairly common technique used to insure proper choral tone: The inner smile. Once while working with a youth chorus, I experienced an odd frustration. I knew that I was communicating clearly, and yet, try as I might, I could not get the singers to express joy. I tried again and again, even resorting to the basic suggestion of jump-starting their connection with a smile. Finally, one of the singers raised their hand. "Our director doesn't want us to smile." At that, the director quickly chimed in, "That's right. We don't smile. We do the 'inner smile' instead, where we lift the inside of our mouths and our cheeks. But the outer face does not smile, except for our eyes." The mystery was solved.

Since the director was open to new ideas, we did some experimenting by having the choir members sing with either the inner or the outer smile. Eventually, the director admitted that he liked the added expressiveness that the outer smile made possible. But I was intrigued with this concept of the inner smile, and have done MUCH research on it in particular, and vocal technique in general. Here's what I've discovered:

The definition of the inner smile is illusory; there are actually lots of definitions.

A few authors and teachers describe it the same way as the director quoted above—no outer smile, cheekbones and inside of the mouth lifted. Some say that the upper lip lifts, showing *some* of the upper front teeth. Some say it lifts, showing *lots* of upper teeth. Others say that the upper lip lifts *off* the front teeth, but does not lift *up* (think air cushion between lip and teeth). Or, it lifts both up *and* off. Some include raising the eyebrows as part of the technique. Many who discuss the inner smile talk about the surprise mouth position, as in, "Say 'Ah!' while acting surprised."

Vocal Technique

If the inner smile definition is somewhat hard to pin down, the definition of the "correct" or "best" method of singing is impossible to grasp.

Some say that the upper teeth must be covered completely by the upper lip. Others claim that the upper teeth should be *visible* at all times. Still others assert that the *bottom* teeth should be covered by the bottom lip. Some state that the face should be totally slack, with no muscles engaged at all except for those muscles needed to hoist the jaw up and down. Others claim that the mouth should be open about an inch for most singing. Some say it should be open as wide as possible. Some experts and teachers say the tongue should be relaxed. Some say the tongue should be pulled back. Pushed down. The tip of the tongue touching the bottom front teeth. Making an arch. The nostrils flared. *Not* flared. And the larynx should be in the neutral position. The *high* position. The *low* position.

Breathing Methods

Well, how about breathing? What of that?

Some experts claim that the abdominal wall should be held out during the exhalation. Others state that the abdominal wall should move *in* during the exhalation. The entire area of lower ribs, stomach and back should expand and contract. *Only the tummy* should expand and contract. On the staccato pulse, the stomach should move *out*. No, it should move *in*. Imagine the breath going out the top of your head. Focused like a laser in front of your teeth. Spinning in the back of the mouth.

Tone

And what of the tone?

The singing voice should be resonant and have a similar timbre all the way through the range. No, it should be dark. Light. Brilliant. Rich. Versatile. "Blending" (if you're a choral singer). No, choral singers should be "excellent" singers, period.

In conclusion, after all my research, one thing is clear. I can say, with absolute certainty that... NOTHING IS CLEAR! It is nearly impossible to conclude anything other than, "People believe what they believe, and I'm sure they have excellent reasons for believing it." There seem to be almost as many theories and ideas as there are teachers! What's a singer or director to do?!

Combining Truth and Beauty

Even though the study of vocal technique presents quite a perplexing potpourri of pedagogical possibilities, there is at least one technique that allows for both truth and beauty of choral tone. This technique takes many of its tenets from the lists above, and I recommend it to you as only ONE possibility. But, like I said, this is not a book on vocal technique. While I endorse the technique briefly described below, I only do so because I know firsthand that it allows for truthful expression while producing a beautiful tone *and* a healthy, effective voice. I support and encourage any technique that does the same thing. Unfortunately, many directors do singers a disservice by requiring a technique that actually *prevents* them from being successful soloists—soloists must be expressive.

The Road to "The Inner Smile"

The notion of the inner smile evolved for a good reason—to prevent unnecessary tension and "spreading" (the excessive brightening of vowels). This makes sense, since singing with a *wide and narrow* smile will produce a rather tight and strident tone. The other choral phenomenon the inner smile hopes to prevent is that of voices not blending because they're "sticking out." This will occur if a few singers are spreading while others are not. (Ironically, many Baltic women's choruses have a very uniform sound because they are all spreading and producing the same bright vowels!)

The Outer Smile that Sounds Good

In technical terms: If you allow the singers to engage their zygomaticus minor muscle while not overly engaging the risorious or zygomaticus major, they can engage the muscles necessary for truthful expression without compromising the tone.

In less technical terms: If you allow the singers to lift the upper lip (without pulling the lips too far sideways or too far up), they can engage the muscles necessary for truthful expression without compromising the tone

In lay terms: If the song calls for joyful connection, allow the singers to smile, but smile up more than out. This will keep them connected while maintaining beauty of tone. (Forcing the jaw downward, however, or opening the mouth unnaturally wide will interfere with both expression and a naturally beautiful tone.) When singers connect to other emotions, their lips can be flexible and adaptable to their emotional and vocal needs in the moment. If the singers are connected and not hampered by any particular vocal technique, their lips will respond appropriately. According to distinguished teacher and author Richard Miller, when singers engage the zygomatics they actually enhance the tone as it helps them maintain a uniform timbre throughout their range. It also allows for truthful expression.

The Emotion Muscles

My experiences as a singer, coach, teacher, and scholar have led me to this conclusion: The zygomaticus major and minor are The Emotion Muscles. When they are allowed to function naturally in reaction to the brain's electrochemical signals and the concurrent thoughts and feelings, the singer has access to emotions. When these muscles are not allowed to contract, the singer loses virtually all emotional connection to the music. In *Solutions for Singers: Tools for Performers and Teachers*, Miller suggests this when he writes of the zygomaticus major:

> Its participation in facial expression is determined by the emotion to be expressed. [He adds] The zygomatics can remain elevated even during expressions of contempt or disdain.

I would go one step further and say that the zygomatics must be in some state of elevation or dynamic movement if we are to connect to powerful emotions when we sing. The only possible exception might be expressions of "dumbfoundedness" or "shock." In those cases, the synonymous phrase

"I'm stunned" might just as well describe the brain's state of temporary electrochemical shut-down. That sort of emotional overwhelm creates a "shut-down" brain which then results in a "shut-down" face. When the lyrics and music support this slack- jawed state of shock, a matching mental, emotional, and physical state is appropriate. With most music, however, our thoughts, feelings, faces, and voices are expressing other emotions.

Because of this, any vocal technique that prevents or unnaturally manipulates the zygomaticus muscles' involvement is a technique that interferes with passionate singing. This would include the slack jaw (or idiot jaw) technique as well as the inner smile, both of which disconnect the singer from emotional truth.

With all due apologies to the late Ogden Nash, here is the poetic version of this prose.

> Expression will be automaticus
> If you engage both zygomaticus.
> No? Prepare to be emotionally flaticus.

♦ An Exercise for You or The Choir

Try the surprised "Ah!" but add to the surprise that it's your birthday, and your best friend just came to the door—your best friend you thought was 3000 miles away. Allow your sense of joy to express itself in your lips, smiling and lifting but without spreading. Now sing *Alleluia!* Depending on your own facial structure, you might be easily and naturally showing lots of teeth, or just some teeth, when you sing with this technique. You might notice if your upper lip juts out slightly from the top teeth. (Extending the lips to their *extreme* position, like a megaphone, creates an unnatural tone with most vowels, and interferes with truthful expression.)

Now try it again but use one of the disconnecting techniques. Relax your jaw and lips, making sure that they stay relaxed. If you try the idiot jaw technique, let everything south of your cheekbones just hang there, as if you'd been given shots of Valium directly into your cheeks, lips, and jaw. If you want to try the inner smile, smile only with your eyes and the inside of the mouth and cheeks. Resist all temptations to actually smile (don't elevate the sides of the mouth), but do lift the upper lip slightly along with your cheeks and eyes. Now sing *Alleluia!* How do you feel? Which method allows your joy to naturally flow? Try singing any *Alleluia* that you know using both techniques. What differences do you notice? How about with a phrase such as "I don't like you!" Notice what your face naturally does when you speak that phrase, spitting it out with appropriate venom. Now sing it that way, using the "Alleluia" melody. Sing it again, but only "express" with the insides of the mouth, the cheeks, the artificially lifted upper lip, and the eyes. When you sing with an unnatural and disconnected expression from nostrils down, what does that do to your sense of truth, connection, and conviction? How does it affect the intensity of your feelings?

Tongue Position

A "home" tongue position that helps prevent unnecessary tension (while allowing unfettered expression and a beautiful tone) is to have the tip of the tongue barely touching the bottom teeth, with half of it visible above the teeth. Such a tongue position will help create a pleasing resonance that "cuts through" an orchestra and blends with other voices. It also helps to keep the tongue relaxed, and releases pressure from the back of the throat and the larynx. If they combine this with "the outer smile that sounds good," (for joyful connection), and the consistently-engaged-and-in-flux zygomatics during most other singing, the singers will have a technique that can honor both the composer's intent and your sense of aesthetics.

Experts on Expression

I'm convinced that directors who advocate the inner smile or the idiot jaw technique have a positive intention—their main goal is to insure that the choir sounds great. The director who wouldn't let his singers smile was trying to insure a beautiful tone, but he unknowingly insured a lack of presence in their faces (and bodies) by disconnecting the singers from their own neuropsychobiological truth. By preventing certain expressions on their faces and bodies, he negated electrochemical exchanges in the brain—he almost literally "short-circuited" their soul connection.

In his seminal text *On the Art of Singing*, Richard Miller writes about technique and emotional expression:

> Singing machines are uninteresting. The only reason for developing a stable vocal technique is to be able to communicate sound and emotion to the listener.

> It is as essential for the singer to learn the language of the body and the impact of facial expressions as it is to learn how to accomplish the even vocal scale.

> Dramatic training is as essential to the singer as to the actor. Before dismissing any vocally talented singer as lacking in "imagination," the

teacher should explore the technical routes available for the externalization of internal emotion.

Even though you don't intend to do so, you might be advocating vocal techniques that prevent this "externalization of internal emotion." If Miller's words and the possibility of alternative vocal techniques don't entice you away from a Tone Trumps Truthful Expression paradigm, the following might.

In the book, *A Spectrum of Voices: Prominent American Voice Teachers Discuss the Teaching of Singing*, author Elizabeth Blades-Zeller interviews 20 master teachers. In those interviews, the following five points are made consistently by these leaders in the field.

1. The primary goal of any singer is to communicate the composer's intention, and engage the audience.

2. Singers can not engage either themselves or the audience if their vocal technique gets in the way of their human connection and expression.

3. It is important to sing with a vibrant and expressive face.

4. Singers are advised to study the Alexander Technique, a method of body work stressing relaxation as a precursor to expression. Experts in the Alexander Technique agree that the face will and should be naturally expressive, including smiling, if the singer is connected and relaxed.

5. In order to do their best work, singers need a supportive environment that will enable them to be genuinely expressive.

Truthful Connection is Flexible

Incorporating truthful connection principles early in the rehearsal process allows you many opportunities to adjust the singers' technique if their expression is creating a sound that you don't like. For example, if their vowel is too bright on a particular word because of their facial expression, it's very easy to guide them to match vowels, open their mouths a little wider, or smile tall rather than wide. "Your connection is awesome, folks. You just need to be careful on that one word." If their connection seems to be too intense for that section, you can ask them to tone that down as well. Combining the work on truthful connection with attention to choral sound will result in a gorgeous, vibrant sound and presence that impacts audiences much more than if you focus on sound to the detriment of connection.

A choral adjudicator once told me that she was shocked when she saw the difference between one group's performance of two different songs. The first was a show choir number, full of energy and expression. She went up to the director and raved about the group. Later at the festival, the choir sang again. This time they performed a traditional choral piece, done in traditional formation. Surprisingly, they were deadly dull and boring, with no expression. The adjudicator described them as "standing like trees—their vibrant, energized choral tone now bland."

This approach to performance unfortunately occurs in choirs at all levels. Take a look at this review of a professional British choir that specializes in Renaissance music. The reviewer, Rebekah Ahrendt, wrote:

> …Which brings me to my biggest beef about this concert. How much perfection can one endure? [The director], who founded the [group], is an exacting taskmaster who has established a solid international reputation for his group of fabulously trained singers. Their intonation is impeccable, their performances are without technical flaw, and their voices are lovely. But I felt like I was listening to a recording. Perhaps the lack of vital energy in the concert was a by-product of traveling long distances. Perhaps it is the result of audiences who expect CD-quality performance. Whatever the cause, I came away feeling a little disappointed that I was not transported from my seat by the power of polyphony. Through the program we had journeyed across the entire Renaissance, but somehow it all looked a bit the same.

While this is but one review, many people have similar opinions about choral music. They often choose not to even attend concerts, because experience tells them that they won't be "transported," they won't experience "vital energy," and everything will look "a bit the same." They stay home, because they are sure that if they go to the concert, they will be "disappointed." How unnecessary and completely reversible a phenomenon this is.

Movement: The Willow, Not the Oak

Some directors believe that choral singers need to stand still, tall and straight, moving neither body, limb, nor head. This belief, like that of the inner smile, is well-intended but misguided, and actually limits the singers' vocal and physical expression, as it impedes their emotional connection.

The core ideas behind such beliefs are that singers must "stand tall" to have a solid foundation for their breathing and singing, and they must be still so as not to distract the audience from the visual homogeneity of the choir. It is true that a slouching or off-balance singer will be less able to project. And if singers are moving independently, the audience will lose that sense of the choir being "one body." Closer inspection, however, reveals the fallacies of this approach. The unifying factor in choral singing is our humanity, not our uniformity. And the notion that only a "still" singer will have vocal support is not accurate—the body of a fully connected singer will be thoroughly engaged in coordination with the mind. It will have all the muscular/skeletal support it needs for powerful singing as it moves in response to thoughts and feelings. Researchers like Babette Lightner and David Gorman are helping us realize that the body always reflects and supports our thoughts and feelings. The truth is that our bodies will naturally find their most effective and efficient alignment—if we are truthfully engaged and if our directors encourage this process, while saying nothing to discourage it.

Body positions consistent with those of truthfully connected singers include the following: Feet tend to be about shoulder-width apart, knees relaxed, weight on the balls of the feet, with the torso relaxed, expanded, and flexible. A feeling of vitality infuses them, with no body part feeling locked or rigid. Their bodies move fluidly, in tandem with their hearts and minds.

Here are but a few of the infinite possible movements to model and help singers explore as natural external responses to their internal process.

- The head moving slowly and slightly side to side when connecting to and expressing the sublime or beautiful.
- The head moving slightly up then down with assertion or anger.
- The head tilting slightly or moving side to side when connected to feelings of love or adoration.
- The head tipping slightly back then down again when the singers connect to something amusing or ridiculous.
- The torso twisting or swaying slightly (the arms moving freely with it) in response to a lyrical/tender thought or intense emotion.

♦ Exercise for the Choir

Ask each singer to place their right hand on the shoulder of the singer below them and to the right of their "window," and their left hand on the shoulder of the singer to the left. As the choir sings, have them move the two singers below them gently with the music. (Make sure that all are standing with feet about shoulder-width apart, with one foot slightly forward.) Stop. Now have the entire choir move on their own power. Next, as they sing, have them switch from still body to connected body, still head to connected head. This exercise helps singers discover the brain/body connection, expanding their emotional range. Note: *Move with the meaning, don't bounce to the beat.*

Be the Bunny

Once upon a time, there were several choral directors who presented the song *Little Bunny Foo Foo* to their singers at a music camp. Their performances were terrifically engaging—lively, joyful, expressive, full of fun. They were definitely connected to the heart and soul of *Little Bunny Foo Foo*.

The most significant aspect of their performance? HUGE SMILES (the outer kind) were beaming from their faces throughout the song. Of course, the song would have failed miserably without those smiles.

Here's the point. When you think about the amount of deep human meaning in a typical camp song, you're bound to conclude that it pales in comparison to that in most choral literature. And yet, many directors want their choirs to sing with less expression than the *Little Bunny Foo Foo* singers. The argument that putting that much expression into choral music would sacrifice tone has some merit—after all, the expression of *Little Bunny Foo Foo* IS more important than its tone, especially in a sing-a-long venue. However, in today's choral world, many directors find it far too easy to sacrifice expression on the altar of "perfect" tone.

The Road to Uninspiring Music is Paved...

Directors who advocate a certain pedagogy that stifles expression may have an admirable goal—to insure that the singers' technique doesn't get in the way of their beautiful and blended sound. Even though their intentions are positive, such directors would serve their choir and its audiences well to reconsider this practice. The insistence on the inner smile, the idiot jaw—or any other technique which precludes truthful expression—not only trumps that expression, it prevents it altogether. It prevents the singers from connecting to their own emotional core, impedes their growth as soloists, and negates the singer-to-audience connection that is so vital for the choral arts.

New Paradigm

The time has come for a paradigm shift. Choral artists can combine truth and beauty, and have more of each as a result. The rest of the book will present the techniques you can use with your singers to help them be as expressive as those directors performing *Little Bunny Foo Foo*—even if the choir is "only" singing Handel's *Messiah*, the *Carmina Burana*, or the Mozart *Requiem*.

4

Analyze the Text

When you are describing
A shape, or sound, or tint;
Don't state the matter plainly,
But put it in a hint;
And learn to look at all things
With a sort of mental squint.

Lewis Carroll, *Poeta Fit, Non Nascitur*

The first step of the truthful connection process is Text Analysis. This can be straightforward, or it can lead you on circuitous routes before it brings you to an interpretation that you like. Either way, since authors often "don't state the matter plainly," your looking at the text "with a sort of mental squint" will frequently bring unexpected rewards.

Text Analysis Questions

1. What is the main subject matter?

2. Is the meaning clear throughout the entire piece? Does every word and passage make total sense?

3. Might there be some figurative language (such as metaphor, simile, personification, irony or symbol) which is not obvious upon first reading? If figurative language seems to be present, what might its meaning be? Might the entire text be a metaphor for something else?

4. What is the theme, and how does the composer feel about it?

5. Does the composer's music and setting of the text support your interpretation of theme?

6. How does the title support your interpretation? What does it mean or relate to?

7. Who is the speaker? Is the speaker defined clearly?

8. Who is the speaker addressing? Is that clear?

9. Who wrote the lyrics? Are they original or do they come from another source?

10. In what social, cultural, personal, or historical context were the lyrics written?

After answering all these questions once, look at your answers again. Do you still agree with your previous answers, or have you learned something that will lead you to new conclusions?

Inspect the Text For the First Time

Take a look at the lyrics for *You Are the New Day,* the very popular song recorded by The King's Singers.

You Are the New Day
By John David, Arranged by Peter Knight

You are the new day.
I will love you more than me
And more than yesterday
If you can prove to me you are the new day.

Send the sun in time for dawn,
Let the birds all hail the morning.
Love of life will urge me say,
You are the new day.

When I lay me down at night knowing we must pay,
Thoughts occur that this night might stay yesterday.
Thoughts that we as humans small
Could slow worlds and end it all
Lie around me where they fall
Before the new day.

One more day when time is running out for everyone,
Like a breath I knew would come
I reach for a new day.
Hope is my philosophy,
Just needs days in which to be,
Love of life means hope for me,
Borne on a new day.
You are the new day.

Used by permission, © Warner Bros. Publications

What is the main subject matter?

On first reading it appears to be a song about love, perhaps one person's love for another.

Is the meaning clear throughout the entire piece? Does every word and passage make total sense? If they don't, what questions do you have?

No. While most of it makes sense, some of it is confusing.

Why does the person spoken to need to "prove" to the speaker that they are "the new day"?

What must the two of them "pay" for? How might this night "stay yesterday"?

What does the speaker mean when they speak of ending "it all"? How is time running out "for everyone"?

Might there be some figurative language (such as metaphor, simile, personification, irony, symbol) which is not obvious upon first reading? If figurative language seems to be present, what might its meaning be? Might the entire text be a metaphor for something else?

There might be some figurative language. Could "You are the new day" be a metaphor, comparing "you" to "the new day"? Or, could the entity being sung to be literally "the new day"? If so, this would be similar to personification, and not a metaphor. If interpreted this way, "you" and "the new day" would be the same thing. "You" IS "the new day."

What is the theme, and how does the composer/lyricist feel about it?

Good grief, I don't know! If "you" IS the "new day," and not a person, then perhaps this isn't a love song. If that is the case, the theme might be more related to the "new day" than to the loved one. And what about all those literal words that don't make sense yet? Nope. There are just too many unknowns at this point to declare a theme.

Does the composer's music, and their setting of the text, support your interpretation of theme?

I couldn't say as I'm still not comfortable defining the theme.

How does the title support your interpretation? What does it mean or relate to?

I'm still not sure. It could be a love song to a person, or to "the new day." I need to figure this out before I can come up with a theme.

Who is the speaker? Is the speaker defined clearly?

The speaker is not defined clearly.

Who is the speaker addressing? Is that clear?

The only thing I can figure is that they are either singing to a person or a "day."

Who wrote the lyrics? Are they original or do they come from another source?

John David. That's all I know.

In what social, cultural, personal, or historical context were the lyrics written?

I have no idea. I see no clues about any of this.

At this point, many questions have yet to be answered. None of the later answers help with the earlier ones, so it's time for closer inspection. This is also the point where it can get to be really fun.

Text Analysis: *Round Two*

Start by doing all you can to answer the questions about author and context. This will hopefully give you some kind of framework upon which to hang your other answers. I always like to start with the internet. If I'm still unsure after that, I try and contact an expert via email, or head to the library or bookstore.

In researching this on the internet, I found a discussion board claiming that John David was a British soldier in the Falklands conflict, and that the song is an anti-war song. This is interesting information that could put the missing pieces together. To check for accuracy, the next step was to get in touch with an "expert." Since The King's Singers popularized this song and continue to sing it today, I contacted one of their members (David Hurley) via their website and received the following response.

New Day was originally performed by a little known 60s/70s British pop group called Airwave (and I think John David was one of the members). As a result it does pre-date the Falklands conflict by a few years. Having said that, there is a somewhat strong pacifist sentiment in the text, and we have always viewed it as an anti-bomb song with slightly hippy overtones! It is amazing how up-to-date the words are, and their relevance seems all the more important in these difficult times.

And with those bits of research and correspondence, the pieces can fall into place. Take a look at the text again.

You Are The New Day
By John David, Arranged by Peter Knight

You are the new day.
I will love you more than me
And more than yesterday
If you can prove to me you are the new day.

Send the sun in time for dawn,
Let the birds all hail the morning.
Love of life will urge me say,
You are the new day.

When I lay me down at night knowing we must pay,
Thoughts occur that this night might stay yesterday.
Thoughts that we as humans small
Could slow worlds and end it all
Lie around me where they fall
Before the new day.

One more day when time is running out for everyone,
Like a breath I knew would come
I reach for a new day.
Hope is my philosophy,
Just needs days in which to be,
Love of life means hope for me,
Borne on a new day.
You are the new day.

What is the main subject matter?

Now it is clear that the main subject matter is not love, but rather our hope for a future without nuclear destruction or cataclysmic war.

Is the meaning clear throughout the entire piece? Does every word and passage make total sense? If they don't, what questions do you have?

The meaning is now clear. The speaker is fervently hoping for the new day to arrive. If the new day does arrive, it means the world still exists, and mankind still has the possibility of a viable future.

Humans "must pay" for their mad rush towards nuclear armament, and for their tendency to solve conflict through war.

Ending "it all" refers to nuclear annihilation. Our time is running out to stop extinction via "the Bomb." With nuclear proliferation occurring at a frantic pace (in the 60's and 70's), time did indeed appear to be "running out." The song is probably just as relevant today, if not more so.

Might there be some figurative language (such as metaphor, simile, personification, irony, symbol) which is not obvious upon first reading? If yes, what might its meaning or subtext be?

Yes, "you" is possibly referring to "the new day." "New day, please be here when I wake up," the speaker could be saying. "You" could also be the audience, since one of the tenets of the Peace Movement was personal responsibility. ("Let there be peace on earth, and let it begin with me.") I think I'll put it to a vote and let the choir decide which interpretation they like best.

What is the theme, and how does the composer/lyricist feel about it?

The theme is, "We are very close to destroying the Earth and all of humankind. But with each new morning we awake, there is hope for a different future." The author, though clearly concerned, is still optimistic. If "you" is the audience, the theme is, "We need to do what we can to insure there is a new day."

Does the composer's music, and their setting of the text, support your interpretation of theme?

John David (and arranger, Peter Knight) have created a very lyrical and harmonious piece of music. This supports the theme of hope "borne on a new day." It also adds a sweetness that coincides with the way the author feels about life. In addition, there is a highlighted, almost breathless quality when the sopranos drop out during, "Send the sun in time for dawn, let the birds all hail the morning," and "Thoughts that we as humans small could slow worlds and end it all." This makes sense, since these are the two most important and portentous phrases. The first sentence is the fervent plea for the new day to be there in the morning, and the second is the clearest warning to the listener of the peril we're in. The fact that the sopranos drop out could symbolize mankind's self-destruction and potential absence from this gorgeous planet.

How does the title support your interpretation? What does it mean or relate to?

You Are The New Day. The author loves the personified "new day," and for good reason. As long as it exists, so does he; and so do we. If "you" is the audience, the song becomes a direct "call to arms" concerning everyone's personal responsibility to "wage world peace."

Who is the speaker? Is the speaker defined clearly?
The speaker could easily be any one of us. It could also be John David.

Who is the speaker addressing? Is that clear?
The speaker is either addressing "the new day," the audience, or perhaps both at different times. The choir will decide. As we continue to refine our interpretation, we might imagine we're singing to a specific world leader—someone who might need to hear this plea and be able to do something about it.

Who wrote the lyrics? Are they original or do they come from another source?
John David, a member of the British band, "Airwaves," wrote the original lyrics.

In what social, cultural, personal, or historical context were the lyrics written?
John David wrote these lyrics during the 60's or 70's, a time of significant political and social upheaval and concern with nuclear annihilation, personal responsibility, and world peace.

Post Analysis

Once you are comfortable with the analysis of your literature, present your thoughts to the choir. Sharing your thoughts will usually have a positive impact on the group, helping them to create a unified and cohesive interpretation. The exercises at the end of this chapter can help them to clarify further.

Text analysis is important even when the song's meaning seems obvious. Going through the above steps will often lead you to information that will surprise you, helping you and the singers immensely.

Religious Text Analysis

Songs with any sort of religious significance give testimony to the necessity of analysis. Whenever you are working with a religious text, check the source and look at its context as this will often lead you to key insights. When doing research for Aaron Copland's *At the River,* for example, I learned that the text concerned the apocalypse (mentioned in the Bible). This meaning informed the entire analysis of the piece, and led to a very satisfying "meeting" of text and music. The interpretation became: "Individuals slowly come to terms with, and eventually rejoice en masse after learning that the world is ending. They start in their homes or places of work, then gradually meet friends and family as they head for the river and eternal bliss."

Another reason to be especially vigilant with religious texts is that they often have critical symbolism, the meaning of which is elusive until you do the research. And if these are not sufficient reasons to look with a "mental squint," consider the fact that many phrases in spirituals have double meanings related to slavery. Arthur C. Jones' book, *Wade in the Water: The Wisdom of the Spirituals*, discusses this in great detail and would be an invaluable resource for anyone directing spirituals.

If you don't do the research, you might be putting yourself and the singers at a significant disadvantage. I once worked with a choir that was rehearsing Brian Tate's *Gate Gate*, a song with a Buddhist text relating to the philosophy of Non Attachment (living in a state of profound peace and acceptance—no matter what). Immediately before working with the group on that piece, I asked the director if she would like to explain the meaning, or if she'd prefer me to do it. "I don't know what it means. I'm doing it because I liked the way it sounded when I heard it at a music reading session," she confessed *sotto voce*. While liking the music is an excellent reason to choose it, it only marks the beginning of the director's involvement. The preparation I had done included finding translations of the piece, understanding the function of the text in the context of Buddhism, and clarifying the meaning of Non Attachment for teenage singers. This work was relatively easy and very interesting. More importantly, it was necessary—it enabled the singers to understand the deeper meaning of the text, and it empowered them to relate to it on a personal level.

◆ Exercise for the Choir: *Operative Words*

The purpose of this exercise is to help singers understand how word emphasis relates to interpretation, meaning, and expression. This exercise will help to unify the interpretation right away and save you lots of time and effort during subsequent rehearsals.

The singers work in small groups, each preparing separate sections of the text. (If the text is relatively short, each group could analyze it in its entirety.) The members within each group reach consensus about which words should receive emphasis in order to communicate the intended meaning, rehearse their "choral reading," and then present their interpretation to the group. They may choose to also share the justifications for their choices.

Once they present their interpretation, open it to the group for feedback. Does everybody agree? Is there any discussion to be had? Once all thoughts are aired and any disagreements resolved, the presenting group stands in front and leads the entire choir in the "choral reading" of that text. The rest of the group has paid close attention to which words are operative (perhaps marking the score), and joins in accordingly.

Whether you do so before, during, or after the group presentations, it is often helpful to lead the group in stressing different words to see how the meaning changes.

◆ An Exercise for the Choir: *Living Lyrics*

The purpose of this exercise is to engage as many areas of the brain as possible so as to deepen and enrich the connection to text, especially for singers who learn best through movement or social interaction.

If a text is of reasonable length (24 or fewer lines), give it to groups of 6 to 12 singers. Have them create a "living sculpture" of the text in which they incorporate movement along with spoken vocalization. The only guidelines are that their creation attempt to depict the text's meaning, and all elements must be created with their bodies and voices (no props or set pieces). The whole choir (in different groups) could work on the same piece, or you could give different pieces to the different groups. You could also break a very large piece into workable sections, assigning each to different groups. While the most learning occurs in the performers, the watchers will also gain insights. Give them enough time to brainstorm, experiment, and practice. This could be done in 15 to 45 minutes, depending on the length and complexity of the piece. When they're ready, they present to the group.

To give you a better sense of what this can look like, here are a few different possibilities: The group moves or speaks in unison/different people in the group move or speak at different times. Key words are acted out/themes and concepts are acted out. The movements are attempts at realism/the movements are impressionistic.

The great fun here is that the singers combine their vocal, physical, and imaginative powers to create something unique—an embodiment of the text that will bring richness to their understanding, a passion to their connection, and more expressiveness to their singing. It's a lot of fun as well, and will help to develop a sense of community.

5

Plot & Character

Like every other form of art, literature is no more and nothing less
than a matter of life and death. The only question worth asking
about a story—or a poem, or a piece of sculpture, or a new
concert hall—is, "Is it dead or alive?"
Mavis Gallant, "What Is Style?" Paris Notebooks

I have discovered that we may be
in some degree whatever character we choose.
Besides, practice forms a man to anything.
James Boswell, London Journal (1762)

Once you do the basic text analysis, you are on solid footing for the next
phase—helping the singers create a Plot and a Character that will live in
their imaginations. While not all songs lend themselves to this technique,
many will have an obvious plot—and some a clear character—"built in" to
the lyrics.

Fair Phyllis I Saw
Madrigal by John Farmer (1599)

Fair Phyllis I saw sitting all alone,
Feeding her flock near to the mountain side.
The shepherds knew not whither she was gone,
But after her lover Amyntas hied: .
Up and down he wander'd while she was missing;
When he found her, O then they fell a-kissing,
O then they fell a-kissing.

Summarize the Plot

Someone saw the shepherdess, Phyllis, sitting all alone and feeding her flock.
The shepherds didn't know where she was, and Amyntas searched for her
everywhere. When he found her they kissed passionately.

Some directors see a bawdy *double entendre* in this text. Generally speaking, if you have solid analytic support for such an interpretation—and the

singers and audiences are ready for it—make the choice. The word painting technique of the English Madrigal school (in which the music "paints" the same picture as the text) definitely supports "up and down" as referring to Amyntas's search for Phyllis. If you decide it means something more, you would be supported by the sociocultural milieu of the Renaissance, even if you could find no direct statement that the text was written with that interpretation in mind.

Identify the Setting

Phyllis and Amyntas are shepherdess and shepherd in Virgil's poem, *The Eclogues*. It was written in 37 B.C. and seems to be set in the same period. Virgil was Roman, therefore the singers could safely assume that the setting was the Roman countryside. Where exactly? It doesn't matter that much (except for the fact that it needs to have "up and down" hills), but it would be good to show the singers some pictures of the Italian landscape, and perhaps some paintings of the period which include shepherds and shepherdesses. (The internet is a great source.) Even though the singers don't need to know the actual name of the area, they do need to create a specific mental picture of the setting. (More on this in the next chapter.)

Establish Your Identity

Who is speaking? The only clue is that the person who was watching the shepherdess is the one describing what happened. The first-person "I" in "I saw fair Phyllis..." makes this clear. What the lyrics do not make clear is *specifically* who this person is.

In such a situation, the singers get to use their imagination to create the character's identity. (Some singers might initially balk at this, but will usually come to relish the creative empowerment.) The person watching could be anyone who had reason to be on the mountainside that day. They could be an admirer of Phyllis, another shepherdess, a hiker, or any number of other people. It is probably not another shepherd, however, because a shepherd would not have referred to his fellows as "the shepherds." He might have referred to them as "we," or "the other shepherds," but not "the shepherds." So, the possibilities are almost endless, and also tempered by the time period and setting.

To help narrow down the choices, look at how the character describes the event. This speaker describes it matter-of-factly, without an extreme amount of emotional content. While there are no direct textual clues, the absence of these is a clue in itself—the speaker is probably NOT a spurned lover of Phyllis. If they were, the text would indicate their upset.

Another way to narrow the choices is to examine the mood of the music. *Fair Phyllis* is light, joyful, and "appreciative" of Phyllis' and Amyntas' love (as indicated by the elongated triplet feel of "and then they fell a-kissing"). Knowing that, the character chosen could admire Phyllis and Amyntas, and their love.

Example: I am a 12-year-old admirer of Phyllis who was picking sunflowers for my mother's table when I saw the events unfolding. I could see it all, because I'm on the mountain path that overlooks both Phyllis and the shepherds in the neighboring valleys.

The singers in the choir would need to make a similar decision, but they don't need to make the same one. Their choices can all be different—as long as they fit the mood, the textual clues, and the setting.

Clarify Your Feelings About the Subject Matter

Once the singers have established a character, they would then decide how their character feels about what they are singing. Taking the "12-year-old admirer" as my character, I might clarify my feelings like this:

> I (as in "my character") am absolutely a-giggle about this whole event. I have yet to have a relationship with someone, but something beyond my ken is awakening my interest in the possibility. I adore the fact that Amyntas is so worried about Phyllis that he would rush from one vale to the next, frantically searching for his lover. I adore, also, the beauty of fair Phyllis as she sits under the olive tree and watches her flock. But what I adore most of all is the way Phyllis and Amyntas rushed to each other's arms and began kissing and hugging each other, as if they were hummingbirds who hadn't tasted nectar for weeks.

Speaking in first person will help singers identify with the character. While this might seem a minor point, it is actually very important. If singers refer to their characters in the third person ("he," "she," or "they") they won't be as emotionally vulnerable. "*She* adores" disconnects the singer from the experience—after all, "she" is "not me." "*I* adore" connects.

Shifting Voice

Some songs will include more than one character, or add a narrator to the mix. With these songs the singer needs to differentiate their different roles, but still connect to each. When they sing as narrator, they have a different connection than when they sing as a character, but one that is no less truthfully engaged.

Biography

Occasionally, it is helpful to know more about the character. When singing texts based on Anne Frank's writing, for example, it behooves the singers (and the director) to familiarize themselves with Anne's diary and learn about her life. With songs that require them to be complex characters (whether real or fictional), encourage the singers to answer the following questions when relevant:

1. What is my (character's) name? Age? Gender?

2. Where do I live? Where am I now (during the song)?

3. What is my socioeconomic position?

4. How do I feel about the subject matter expressed?

5. Why do I feel that way?

6. What specific life circumstances have brought me to the point described in the song?

7. How do I feel about love? Politics? Religion? Money? Family?

8. What social, historical, and cultural forces have influenced my life and viewpoints?

9. How do I feel about my family? How did it influence me?

To sing from the self, there must be a "self" present. Defining your character—and singing as that character or as yourself—is a critical part of the process.

Whether singing as self or character, the singer's expressive potential will be enhanced when they know both their identity and the song's plot. If they are unclear about either, they will have difficulty using the other techniques. If they know both, their expression and connection will continue to grow.

Singing as Yourself

With songs that have a more universal (and less specific) text that is delivered in first-person singular, each singer can use themselves as the character. When doing so, it's just as important to make specific choices about setting and situation, but the difference is that a direct line exists between singer and lyrics. When the singers sing "I," they communicate as themselves and not as a character they create. (They don't have to, however. If it works better for them to create a character, more power to them.)

The following is an example of a song written from the first-person perspective.

When You Wore a Tulip
Music by Percy Wenrich, Lyrics by Jack Mahoney

When you wore a tulip, a sweet yellow tulip,
And I wore a big red rose,
'Twas heaven when you caressed me,
'Twas then Heaven blessed me,
What a blessing, no one knows, no one knows.
My darling, you made life cheerie, when you called me dearie,
'Twas down where the blue grass grows.
Your lips were sweeter than julep, when you wore that tulip
And I wore a big red rose.

The plot of *When You Wore a Tulip* involves a simple nostalgic event. Someone wearing a red rose had a memorable experience with someone wearing a tulip. The rose-wearer enjoyed the other's caress, kiss, and the term of endearment "dearie" spoken "where the blue grass grows." While the plot seems basic, the singer choosing to sing as themselves still needs to use imagination to fill in the specifics, but they can also access their own actual past.

I had a college sweetheart—she was wonderful! Her name was Kathy, and when she and I would get together, it didn't matter what we did because we were always present to each other. We laughed, cuddled, talked, or made plans and the world dissolved to reveal just the two of us and our love.

The singer makes the choice of Kathy (from their own life experience) to be the "you" in the text.

If the singer can forge a more direct line from themselves to the truth of the text, that's great. Perhaps the EXACT situation happened to them. (That would be a stretch in this case due to the tulip and rose detail, but you never know!) If the exact situation did happen to them, they have more to remember, and less to imagine. Either way, the specifics need to be strong—just as strong as they would be if the singer were actually remembering a truthful incident with clarity and detail.

> Truth & Imagination captivate equally—
> The brain dances the same steps to both tunes.

6

Words & Pictures

All words are pegs to hang ideas on.
Henry Ward Beecher, *Proverbs from Plymouth* (1887)

A word is dead
When it is said,
Some say.
I say it just
Begins to live
That day.
Emily Dickinson, Untitled Poem (1872?)

Imagery

One of the richest areas for truthful connection is the area of Imagery. As you will see, it can turn a mundane and "silly" song like *When You Wore a Tulip* into a poignant experience.

♦ Exercise for You and the Choir

Play in pairs, designating one person "A" and the other "B." At your signal, the A's talk for 45 seconds, sharing their *detailed* memories of the last weekend. Stop and switch. Now B's share their memories. During the sharing, the listener does not talk at all.

After 45 seconds, ask them to describe their mental process while talking to their partners. After about one minute, pull their attention back to you and ask if anyone saw any "mental movies," any "pictures in their heads." Most will answer affirmatively.

Repeat the entire exercise, but this time replace "weekend memories" with "fantasy vacation." When they're done, ask the same question about "mental movies." Most people will have had that experience here as well. Then ask if anyone had a "picture" involving the other senses. People will often have had this experience, too. This exercise is similar to the one in which the singers alternate speaking and singing. This one, however, is more specifically designed to illuminate imagery and illustrate the point that the brain "can't tell the difference" between imagination and memory—a picture is a picture.

Share the concept and its terminology with the choir. These specific sensory "pictures" in our heads are called, appropriately enough, "images." We have them (in real life) whenever we imagine, fantasize, or remember. Imagery is the process of creating and using these images.

In order to create an authentic experience for themselves and their audiences, when the singer as character sings anything that would naturally be connected to an image, they need to *create the image*. So, when an image is called for in the lyrics, they use their imaginations to "paint" it, using specific sensory details as their palette. Once the image is created, they refer to it every time they sing, thus strengthening it and its connection to the text and the music. Since they sometimes sing as themselves, the images can also spring from their own memories.

Pegs to Hang Ideas On

In our real life cognitive process, the images come first and then the words. We "remember" and then we speak. We "imagine" and then we describe. So, as the imagery is formed in a singer's mind, it becomes like a memory—it can give vivid life to the text. When singers create specific and detailed images during rehearsal, they are building "pegs to hang ideas on." The word "begins to live" when sung, and enables the singer to continue the process of truthful connection to text. The ideas and specific thoughts that the character/singer connects to these images is their Inner Monologue.

♦ An Exercise for the Choir

First Word…

The singers use their hands and bodies to create a representation of the meaningful words they sing. As in the parlor game, Charades, they mime the "important" words. If their text is "This little light of mine…" they might point their finger towards the ground on "this," hold thumb and forefinger close together for "little," strike a match for "light," and point to themselves for "mine."

There is no correct way for them to do any of this, no right or wrong miming. It's an opportunity to connect their physical selves to the text, their whole bodies to the meaning. Those who are kinesthetic learners will appreciate it no end, but all singers will benefit as it connects them to text in a new and potentially impactful way. It also builds different neural pathways in the brain, creates new connections, and gives the singer even more ways to learn and remember.

When you do this exercise, have the singers sing the piece slowly enough (at first) that they have time to do the movements. Once they have done it at that tempo, gradually speed it up. After they do it *a tempo* with the miming, have them think of the miming without doing it. During feedback, singers might say things like, "I felt more connected without even trying," or "The words came alive somehow."

Cooking for One

While we naturally feel emotions when we connect to our inner monologue and imagery, some singers need this connection to be explained further. For these (often more intellectual) singers, this basic "Recipe for Feeling" can help guide them, and can be used with all truthful connection techniques.

The Basic Recipe for Feeling

1. Create the Imagery and Thought that fits the Meaning of the words.
2. Notice or decide HOW YOU FEEL about this Meaningful Imagery or Thought.

Using this basic recipe might still not be enough for some. If they sing about a clear blue lake with a bluebird circling above it, for example, these singers might imbue their imagery with too many left-brain thoughts (exaggerated here for effect).

The lake has predominantly three different shades of blue, ranging from "robin's egg" to "midnight" as described in *The Artist's Way Off Base*, and ranges in temperature from 38 degrees Fahrenheit at a depth of 168 feet, to 54 degrees Fahrenheit at the surface. The bird is the common scrub jay with a wingspan of 140 millimeters, and a weight of 80 grams. It is flying at an altitude of 187 feet above the lake, catching updrafts that lift it at an angle of 37 degrees relative to its horizontal trajectory.

This hypothetical singer has created a very specific mental picture, but one that probably won't connect them to their feelings! They can use their intellect, however, to attune themselves to their emotions. Making the *cerebral* decision of "I am in awe of the lake's reflective beauty, and amazed at the physics that allows the bird to fly" will help them connect to their feelings.

Imagery's Many Benefits

Brain research shows that as we use our imagination to form these mental movies, we are actually building and strengthening neural pathways, and creating an ever-widening structure of links to vast areas of the brain. This is important, and has several ramifications.

First, it enables singers to retrieve their "stored information." When we create images during rehearsals, we can come back to them on subsequent rehearsals. With each revisit, the images are more vivid, supporting the text with increasing ease and power.

As imagery intersects with text and music, their junction creates more "points of access" for us as singers. In other words, we have more ways to think of them, more ways to remember them, more ways to associate them, and more ways to learn them. Our learning curve is now much steeper, and we learn the music and lyrics much faster.

And the good news is just beginning. The more often singers use imagery, the easier it is for them to have "automatic" access to it. Just like an actual memory, the imagery will pop into their heads if they build it during rehearsals. Come performance time, the singers don't have to create the imagery—it is already there, supporting their truthful connection to text.

If we go back to the Composer as Architect/Singer as Builder analogy, we can see that the singer's use of imagery has started to humanize the building. Since each singer has been mixing text and music with the cement of imagery, they have laid a much stronger foundation. The connection with the audience is beginning to have a foundation as well.

And the benefits continue. Since the imagery is so strong by performance time, and can be accessed so easily, it provides one element on which the singer can focus—instead of on the audience. This helps greatly to manage stage fright and nerves. When it's time to sing, the singers can stand on that strong foundation with a relaxed confidence.

The Seven Senses

Encourage the singers to use all seven of their senses whenever possible as they create their images or refresh their memories. Incorporating the senses of sight, sound, smell, touch, taste, gratitude, and awe (the spiritual or intuitive sense) will help their connections be more vivid, and will activate more parts of the brain and body. And of course, the audience will notice.

We are gifted with marvelous brains that can imagine a more complex painting than Michelangelo ever painted, in one billionth of the time. While we sing the phrase, "In these delightful pleasant groves," we can start to build an entire orchard (if that's the "grove" we choose). We can...

- Smell the sweetly decaying fruit on the ground.
- Touch the bark of the tree.

- Taste the crisp sweetness of the first harvest.
- Hear the "tweep" of the sparrows.
- See the trees stretched out in rows around us.
- Be grateful for the many gifts in our lives.
- Be in awe of that Divine Presence that brings such goodness to the world.

Each time we sing a phrase, we can make the images more specific. Build them in layers. What exactly does the fruit smell like? What exactly does the bark feel like? What does the sparrow's "tweep" sound like, exactly? How many trees are there—how far out from you do they extend? What exactly do they look like? (How tall? What is the size and shape of the leaves? The bark color and pattern? What kind of fruit is it? What does it look like, exactly?) How do you feel as you stand in the presence of the divine? Where do you feel it? What does it do to your soul? Your heart?

Imagery and Emotion

A direct line exists between imagery and emotion. When we think about something that brings us happiness, as we "see" it in our mind we start to feel happy. If we think about something that worries us, we start to worry. If we think about something that brings us peace, we start to feel peaceful. The more specific our details, the more intense and nuanced will be the feeling. This works with memories. It also works with the imagination, which engages virtually identical brain activity.

◆ An Exercise for You or the Choir

Going back to the "delightful pleasant groves," pick one of the sensory images. Since the song is clearly about joy and celebration, enjoy or celebrate whatever image you have chosen. For example, if you chose the smell of the decaying fruit, you might enjoy the sweetness that fills your nostrils, loving the way it reminds you of the most aromatic cider. If you chose the touch of the bark, enjoy the thought of its cool and textured surface. Use your imagination to create the specifics of these images. Say the line, "In these delightful pleasant groves" while thinking of that joyful imagery. If you know the madrigal, try singing a few lines, maintaining connection with the imagery. (Here's a refresher: "In these delightful pleasant groves. In these delightful pleasant groves. Let us celebrate, let us celebrate, let us celebrate our happy, happy loves.")

Questions for the Group

What do you notice about your process? Your connection? Your belief? Your sense of actually having lived the experience you sing about?

Build Imagery at Any Time

Singers can use this process of building imagery at any time. They can do it when they're learning notes, working on blend, adjusting vocal technique, memorizing, or phrasing. At the beginning of the process, the brain might need to devote 99% attention to music, and only 1% to imagery—this is to be expected. Then, as more neural pathways are built due to their association, the focus on music and imagery (and all the other expression elements) will become more balanced. Eventually, the brain will be able to "let go," knowing that all the preparation has gotten the singer to the place where they simply inhabit the song, as it inhabits them. When this happens, the composer as architect will be smiling, for the House will be on its way to being well and truly constructed. The audience won't have to wait too long before they get to step in, feeling right at home.

Imagery in Action

When rehearsing *Fair Phyllis* for the very first time, singers' explorations of imagery might "look" like this:

> **Fair Phyllis I saw sitting all alone,**
> *Looks like young Audrey Hepburn / under oak / big white dress billows on ground around her / green thistles / me on mountain path*

> **Feeding her flock near to the mountain side.**
> *50 sheep / big gray boulders / much happy bleating / pine smell*

> **The shepherds knew not whither she was gone,**
> *Shepherds shouting / some echoes / Amyntas running between them*

> **But after her lover Amyntas hied:**
> *Running fast / brown pants / peasant shirt / carries staff / tiny in the distance*

> **Up and down he wander'd while she was missing**
> *Many hills below / stops and starts / more fast running / sun on my back*

> **When he found her, O then they fell a-kissing,**
> *He dropped his staff / Phyllis stood and ran to him / huge hug / they fall to ground / MUCH kissing!*

> **O then they fell a-kissing.**
> *I held my breath / kissing slower, more intense / big smiles, laughing, and more kissing / my face got so warm!*

The Imagery Process Refined

Using a couple of lines from *When You Wore a Tulip*, let's put the imagery process under the microscope and see its potential as the rehearsals progress. Let's say the singers are singing as themselves, but need to create, or perhaps refresh, their imagery. Since the song has a playful and nostalgic tone, the imagery chosen would reflect that. What follows is what one individual singer might come up with, based on their own memories but with necessary details created by the imagination. (The *imaginary* details are in italics.)

> When you wore a tulip, a sweet yellow tulip,
> And I wore a big red rose.

There was this wonderful dance that our dorm put on when we were both freshmen. *Everybody was told to dress as a tango dancer, so I wore this big red rose on the lapel of my rented tux.*

As I entered the hall, I saw this incredibly interesting looking woman with bright red hair *who wore a bullfighter's costume, and had a yellow tulip pinned to her right shoulder pad.* I remember I laughed out loud when I saw her, and she looked at me. Ay carumba!

> 'Twas heaven, when you caressed me,
> 'Twas then Heaven blessed me,
> What a blessing, no one knows, no one knows.
> My darling, you made life cheerie, when you called me dearie,
> 'Twas down where the blue grass grows.
> Your lips were sweeter than julep,
> when you wore that tulip and I wore a big red rose.

After I asked you to dance, we had such a great time—laughing and moving so well together even though we had just met. We danced with no one else that night, and when the dance was done we walked to the commons. *We took off our shoes and walked slowly through the grass turned blue by the moonlight,* each of my senses awakened and blessed by your touch. No one could possibly know the depths of my feelings for you. Then you shocked me. *"Dearie," you whispered,* "kiss me." Fourth of July and Christmas, move over and make way for my happiest day on Earth! Your lips were so sweet, tasting like salt, strawberries, papaya and desire. What a night! How much I loved you!

Concrete images like these create an emotional experience for the singer, an experience very different from the one they would have if their images were general or non-existent. The creation of such imagery can also be highly enjoyable, and its use empowering.

As Rehearsals Continue

Words are the small change of thought.
Jules Renard, Journal, November 1888, Tr. Elizabeth Roget

The singer continues this process of building imagery—creating thoughts, feelings, and a "sensory picture library" that they can access *as if they were that character*. If this seems daunting, bear in mind that engaging the imagination happens much more quickly than it takes to read about it. The imagination SOARS at lightning speed—instantaneously associating, remembering, inventing, picturing, and ultimately connecting us to an infinite complexity of thoughts and feelings. In contrast, the words written throughout the book to represent this interior experience can only C R A W L.

> The singers rehearse specific imagery, thoughts, and feelings.
> They don't memorize more words.

In addition, since the process is cumulative, the layers of sensory information can be created over the entire rehearsal process. Some people actually love to write down all these details, but while this helps build stronger and more specific imagery, it is not absolutely necessary.

The overriding principle here is that there is no "perfect" amount of imagery—whichever images the singers prepare and rehearse (and thus have ready access to) will give them the most truthful connection to text. They don't need to do hours of detail work on each song; the imagination can engage in a millisecond, giving their sense of truth an instant boost.

Caveat: This is not meant to encourage or condone the adding of emotional connection late in the rehearsal process. While it is true that the imagination works quickly, waiting until late in the process will be *much less effective* than starting early. Adding connection at the last minute can add stress to singers who will have too many new elements to focus on that they haven't thoroughly rehearsed. Too much of their attention will go to what should by now be deeply internalized underpinnings, and this can create anxiety for both you and the choir. The singers won't have the easy access to truthful connection that they would have if their specific neural pathways had been strengthening for weeks. Most importantly, you and they will lose the glorious opportunities to meld connection, tone, and musicality during rehearsals—you simply won't have the time if you start the process a week before the concert. And remember, the more and the earlier the singers connect, the faster and more completely the music will be learned.

Caveat to the caveat: No matter when you introduce truthful connection techniques, you will ultimately do more good than harm—even if your concert is the following week. How can this be—isn't this a contradiction? No. Any truthful connection the singers make will impact the audience and their voices more than singing without that connection. It's just that their concert connection will be so much more powerful when it's started on the first day, and then strengthened throughout the entire rehearsal process!

During Performance

The singers now have the beginnings of a truthful frame upon which to hang their words. The thoughts, feelings, and pictures they created during rehearsals are now at their beck and call, helping them to sing with more power, nuance, and self-confidence. The words "begin to live," and the music begins to connect. We're on our way.

7

The Singer Acts

The actions of human beings are governed, more than anything else, by what they want, consciously or subconsciously.

Uta Hagen, *Respect for Acting* (1973)

It is the objective that gives [the actor] faith in his right to come onto the stage and stay there.

Constantin Stanislavski, *An Actor Prepares* (1936)

A choral conservatory asked me to stage a couple of opera choruses that the singers then presented along with their standard repertoire. When they performed the opera choruses the singers were notably expressive, much more so than when performing their choral repertoire. When discussing this expressiveness, one of the directors said, "Those singers had a purpose." In the context of our discussion, he was implying that most choral literature doesn't provide singers with "purpose," so choral singers don't have such opportunities to be expressive. This is a logical conclusion since opera choruses, with their requisite acting and movement, provide an *obvious* purpose for each singer—a purpose rooted in action. I propose a slightly different way of looking at it: The singers in the opera choruses knew their purpose because they had focused on it at great length during rehearsals. Singers in choirs can do exactly the same thing. Choral literature is *full* of purpose—it just needs to be discovered.

Singing Is Acting

The conservatory director used the term, "purpose," but he could have used "goal," "intention," "reason," or "desire," since all have similar meanings in this context. This element is called the Objective, and, like many other techniques discussed in this book, is incorporated in theatre training. While the dramatic arts are rarely associated with choral education, Leon Thurman reminds us in *Bodymind & Voice*, "Song singing is *always* musical theatre. So is choral singing." There is one key distinction: The actor is given the context in which to say their lines—the chorister gets to invent it.

Objectives

In our lives, we are constantly doing something to some desired effect. Our objective is defined as what we are trying to accomplish. When we are alone, we do tasks. We clean a counter, perfect our golf swing, entertain ourselves by reading a novel. Each of these is an objective.

When we interact with others, our objectives take on more varied forms. We try to affect other people by getting them to think, feel, or do something. Our objective is then defined as how we're trying to affect them. Here are some examples:

We want them to **THINK** that their viewpoint on global warming is unjustified. We want them to *believe* that we were where we said we were. We want them to *understand* the Circle of Fifths.

We want them to **FEEL** better after they put a hole in the wall of their new house. We want them to *suffer* after they broke up with us. We want them to *experience a rush of pride* in their accomplishments.

We want them to **DO** the dishes that are stacked up on the counter after a big party. We want them to *leave* us alone. We want them to *loan* us their car. We want them to *laugh*.

To engage our humanness while singing, we need to know our objective; we need to know how we are trying to affect the person (or entity) who is the recipient of our words.

The Other

Having an objective is only part of the tool kit necessary for building this part of the House of Connection. With most choral literature, the singer also benefits by identifying a specific someone they are trying to affect. Who exactly are they singing to?

In actor training, this entity is called the Other. While lyrics might indicate the identity of this person, animal, mineral, vegetable(!), or deity, much of the time they don't. With most songs, the singers need to construct the other using their imaginations. After they do so, they can see the other in their mind's eye, and then project that other in front of them.

The Other's Reaction

As they sing, the singers can use their imagination to create a reaction in the other that supports the singing. When this happens, the singers open themselves to a richer connection; they feel more deeply.

If the other responds the way the singers intend, the singers "win." They will naturally experience that victory and it will affect their mind, body, face, and voice. If the other "stops feeling sad and smiles," for example, singers will feel good—assuming their imagination is specific and complete enough.

If the singer chooses to have the other resist the objective, the singer might "lose." If this happens before the song is over, the singer might feel frustrated, more determined, angry, or amused. If it happens at the end of the song, the singer will likely experience a deeper reaction like sadness. However this reaction plays out, the choir's expressiveness will be stronger, richer, and more human.

The Obstacle

The singer can also create an obstacle that is separate from the other. This could be an inner psychological obstacle like "fear of the other's reaction," or an external obstacle like "being in a church" (when your emotions are high and you have to suppress your voice) or "a hurricane" (when you want to be heard over the howling). The obstacle presents another opportunity for greater brain involvement through richness of imagination—all leading to completeness of belief and even more nuanced expression.

The Story

"Trying to affect the other" will only take a singer a limited distance on the road to full belief. The singer needs to know more. *Why* are they trying to affect the other? What's going on? What drama is taking place that requires them to sing to the other? What's the time and place? What's the story? The imagination can create all this, or the text might lay it out. Either way, this Story will support and justify the interaction between singer and other.

Power Tools

In order to build a solid structure, singers can answer the following questions about their story. If they experiment with different possibilities during rehearsals, they will soon be able to settle on one that engages them most completely.

1. Who might you be singing to and what exactly do they look like?

2. How might you be trying to affect this other person, entity, or object?

3. What's the time and place; when and where are you singing to the other?

4. What specific event sparks your singing? What might be going on with the other that would compel you to speak these words in a way that matches the composer's tone? (Whether the music is playful, serious, or angry, your story should match.)

5. Why is it so important for you to affect the other?

6. Are there any obstacles?

7. How does the other respond to you?

8. How does their response make you feel? (This question only serves as a reminder to "breathe in" or let the other's reaction affect you in the moment. Don't "pre-program" your reactions.)

Raise the Stakes

Any time they try to affect an other, the choir members can make their sense of purpose stronger by raising the stakes. If affecting the other is critical, the singers will connect with much more commitment and ease; it will become much easier for them to sing with passion. If their stakes are low, their passion will be low as well; it will be much easier for them to sing with passion if they have high stakes.

Here are some questions to help singers raise the stakes.

1. Why is it so important for the other to think, feel, or do what you want?

2. What is the worst thing that could happen if you don't achieve your objective?

3. Can you make the objective more important? Can you create a critical objective and story—one that feels like "life and death"?

Building From Scratch

As you begin to apply the concepts of story, objectives, and the other to different songs, you will notice that some songs give you a lot to work with, and some songs require you to invent almost everything. Let's look at three representative examples.

If you find that plot and character are neither defined nor implied, you have found a text that invites you and your singers to use imagination to create the entire story. Let's explore how you might do this.

Listen to a Jubilant Song
Music by Tim Sarsany
Text paraphrased from Walt Whitman

Listen to a jubilant song!
Our spirit sings a jubilant song!
That is to life full of music,
A life full of music,

A life full of concord,
A life full of harmony!

We sing prophetic joys of lofty ideals,
We sing a universal love awaking the hearts of men.
O to have life,
A poem of new joys,
To shout!

Listen to a jubilant song!
Our spirit sings a jubilant song!
A jubilant song that is to life full of music,
Life full of concord,
A life full of harmony!
We sing a song,
A jubilant song!

© *Santa Barbara Music Publishing*

This is a wonderful text, but all it gives us is that one person or group wants some other to "listen to a jubilant song." And while the interpretation could be simplified to "a choir singing a joyful song for the audience," a more engaging choice would create a richer connection.

Analyze the Text

The first order of business when beginning this process with any song is to look closer at the text. Text analysis offers the first glimmer of possibilities, as it calls us to look at the source of Sarsany's text. Whitman's original text (No. 196 in *Leaves of Grass* entitled *Poem of Joys)* is a much more detailed "love song" to the Soul's earthly experience—including joy, suffering, pain, and death. Here is the first stanza in which Whitman sets forth the themes.

O to make the most jubilant poem!
Even to set off these, and merge with these, the carols of Death.
O full of music! Full of manhood, womanhood, infancy!
Full of common employments! Full of grain and trees.

Throughout the poem, Whitman returns to the theme of the great joys of the "uncaged" spirit—the independent and all-embracing soul that is jubilant even during the most trying of times.

O, while I live, to be the ruler of life—not a slave,
To meet life as a powerful conqueror,
No fumes—no ennui—no more complaints, or scornful
    criticisms.
…O joy of suffering!

He also weaves through the poem many images of this joy of suffering. The repetition of these two themes gives us a clue to their importance. The fact that they are excised from Sarsany's text is equally important. Sarsany has clearly shifted the theme to be that of joyful optimism, peace, and love—and away from an all-inclusive celebration that includes our dark and violent side. Sarsany's text builds more on lines like this one.

> O the joy of that vast elemental sympathy which only the human
> Soul is capable of generating and emitting in steady and limitless
> floods.

We now have a clearer sense of the original poem.

Compare and Contrast

The text of Sarsany's piece, while less specific, does incorporate many of the themes of Whitman's original. Sarsany uses one word where Whitman uses hundreds, but the themes of joy, spirit, brotherhood, and love of life are all present. The most important information to glean from analyzing the original text is the overwhelming joy that Whitman found in every aspect of life. The most critical understanding gained from analyzing Sarsany's text in comparison to Whitman's is that Sarsany excludes death, suffering, and war from the list of joys. The other clear difference is that Sarsany has honed in on the "music" element, and writes of singing "a jubilant song," not making "a most jubilant poem."

Investigating the original text offers a wider perspective and allows us to look more closely at possible meanings. It's as if Sarsany had taken a large original and reduced it greatly in size (thus obscuring some of the detail), but then we came along and enlarged it again. By "enlarging it" to its original size, we are able to see the whole more clearly and, by contrasting it with Sarsany's, can illuminate his themes more vividly. This will impact our story.

Creating the Story

Having acknowledged the similarities and differences between the Whitman original and Sarsany's text, we can now create the story by answering the following basic questions. [The brackets indicate references to Sarsany's text.]

What theme or message are you communicating to the other/s?
Life is incredibly joyful when it is filled with harmony, concord, and music.

Do you direct them to do anything?
Yes. "Listen to a jubilant song!"

Based on both the text and the music, what is your mood?
I am jubilant, fervent, and optimistic!

What might you be feeling so strongly about?
See the possibilities below.

Who might you [we] be?
(See below.)

Who might need to hear these messages [about your joyful life and appreciation of harmony, love, and music? Who might need to hear about the joyful nature of the Soul]?
(See below.)

What might be going on in this other's life that would compel you to share these thoughts?
(See below.)

Where might you be when you try to affect the other?
(See below.)

How might you be trying to affect the other?
(See below.)

Possibility #1: You are a singer in a choir that encountered much hostility recently when you went on a "Peace through Music" world tour. Everywhere you sang, people picketed, clamoring against your government. Eggs were thrown, banners were unfurled, shouts were hurled. However, as soon as you started to sing, the protesters quieted down, eventually becoming quite moved by your concert's theme of "universal love." You are now home and are being honored at a state dinner at your nation's capital. The country's leaders and lawmakers are in attendance, and have read about your experiences in the program. Your director has just given an impassioned address to the audience about the importance of peace through loving means—the importance of joy, brotherhood, and concord—not hate, "scornful criticisms," and war. This song is your attempt to turn the hearts and minds of the leaders around. When the song ends, you hope that they will stop acting out of fear, judgment, and insensitivity so the world will truly be a jubilant place, "full of harmony."

Read the text again with that story in mind.

Listen to a jubilant song!
Our spirit sings a jubilant song!
That is to life full of music,

A life full of music,
A life full of concord,
A life full of harmony!

We sing prophetic joys of lofty ideals,
We sing a universal love awaking the hearts of men.
O to have life,
A poem of new joys,
To shout!

Listen to a jubilant song!
Our spirit sings a jubilant song!
A jubilant song that is to life full of music,
Life full of concord,
A life full of harmony!
We sing a song,
A jubilant song!

As you read through the text, did the interpretation bring more meaning to the words? Did certain phrases stand out as making more compelling and complete sense? Did you get a suspended feeling in your solar plexus as you thought, "Oh my gosh, that fits!"? If you did, this story would be worth investigating further in rehearsal. If you felt that the text did not benefit from that particular meaning, try another one.

Possibility #2: You are a singer in a choir, and that choir is presenting a concert. In the audience is a family member who is extremely frustrated with all the negative aspects of life. They are fed up with the increasing violence in the world, with the crime in their neighborhood, with the meanness of their neighbors. Over the last year, they have isolated themselves more and more, until now they almost never leave their house. It was a real struggle to get them to the concert, but you are hoping that they will hear your message and join the choir. While they have a great tenor voice (which the choir needs), your desire is motivated more by your love for them. You want to help them do what you believe will be in their best interest. By the time the song is done, you hope they will be overwhelmed by the message and the group's positive energy. They will then join the choir, shift their attitude, and reclaim all that is positive in their life.

Go back and read the text with this interpretation in mind. Did this story bring more meaning to the text? Did certain phrases stand out as making more complete sense? Did you get the "Wow, this works!" feeling? If you did, *this* story would be worth investigating further in rehearsal.

As you go through this process with your own repertoire, keep brainstorming until you create an interpretation that makes you want "to shout!"

Plot, but Not Much Else

Fair Phyllis I Saw gives us the plot, but no details about who is singing or who they're singing to. This is more than we had with *Listen to a Jubilant Song*, but plot is not nearly enough to develop a compelling connection—we get to employ our creative imagination once more.

> Fair Phyllis I saw sitting all alone,
> Feeding her flock near to the mountain side.
> The shepherds knew not whither she was gone,
> But after her lover Amyntas hied:
> Up and down he wander'd while she was missing;
> When he found her, O then they fell a-kissing,
> O then they fell a-kissing.

Brainstorm # 1: You are that 12-year-old who had previously observed these events in ancient Rome. You just played a game of hide-and-seek with a person you would really like to kiss. You know exactly what they look like in this present moment. When you discover them behind the straw pile in the stable, they say, "What should we do now?" The spark ignites! It's almost time for you to sit down for dinner and send them home, but you really want to kiss them. If you don't, you won't see them for at least two weeks since their family is going to gather their flock at the coast. As you sing, they start to giggle. You feel a little sheepish, wondering what they're laughing at. When you sing, "a kissing," their mouth opens in mock alarm and your stomach falls, but from that point on they pucker and lean ever closer to you. When you finish the song, you get your kiss. Yippee!

Brainstorm #2: You are singing as yourself, taking care of two young neighbors who are 4 and 6 years old. Their parents are at the hospital with their 10-year-old brother who fell and hit his head. The parents called to say that he's going to be OK, but his siblings are still worried. You've been with them for three hours, it's almost their bedtime, and they always get a bedtime story. They're frightened and more than a little grumpy; if they don't get the story when you tuck them in, all pandemonium could break loose. And these little guys have some serious lung power. The spark: "Tell us a story!" Wanting to take their minds off their brother and their missing parents—if only for a minute or two—you start to sing. As soon as you start, they start to yell at you not to sing. Your resolve increases, as does your awareness that they might really benefit from being distracted. As you continue to sing, trying to get them to smile and enjoy the song with you, they look at each other and crack up! When you sing the "up and down" part, they start waving their hands in the air. When you sing, "And then they fell a kissing," they simultaneously erupt in a huge "YUCK!," then giggle like crazy. Success!

Neither of these is the one "correct" story. Again, as you and the singers develop them, ask yourselves, "Is this right for me? Does this work to engage my imagination and belief?"

Plot & Character, but No Story

When You Wore a Tulip gives us more information, but we still need to develop the story. Without doing so, our connection will be incomplete at best.

> When you wore a tulip, a sweet yellow tulip,
> And I wore a big red rose,
> 'Twas heaven when you caressed me,
> 'Twas then Heaven blessed me,
> What a blessing, no one knows, no one knows.
> My darling, you made life cheerie, when you called me dearie,
> 'Twas down where the blue grass grows.
> Your lips were sweeter than julep, when you wore that tulip
> And I wore a big red rose.

Brainstorm # 1: You are in your living room at night, singing to your sweetheart on your anniversary, wanting them to cheer up because they are depressed about how old they are. The spark is that they just said, "Oh honey, I just can't take it!" and they started to sob. The stakes are high because when they cry they usually sink into a deep, painful depression. This is tough because they tend to shut down physically when they feel this way, often not even able to even look at you. As you sing, they slowly open their eyes, and smile at you big time when you sing, "Your lips were sweeter than julep...." You are relieved that they didn't slip into that depression, and you are thrilled that you both can now celebrate your anniversary.

Brainstorm # 2: You might be singing to your sweetheart of old, having just been reacquainted with them after 15 years. You know exactly what they look like. The place is The High Ground, a very fancy club where your high school reunion is being held. You notice a mutual interest, and you want to get back together with them once you learn that they are available. The spark? They look at you and grin, asking, "So, are you married?" The stakes are high because you have been lonely lately, wishing that you could have a serious relationship. This person loves to laugh, and you know that if you can connect to their sense of humor, you have a chance. The obstacle is that you think they might have just seen another old flame, so you've got to act fast.

When you start to sing, they smile immediately, enjoying you immensely. After you croon "My darling" they lead you out to the veranda. Oh boy!

As you apply story to your repertoire, you will undoubtedly find many permutations of plot, character, and the other. Engage the imagination by answering all the pertinent questions, and your singing will soar. After singers in the San José State University Chorale applied the story technique to Mendelssohn's *Drei geistliche Lieder,* director Elena Sharkova was astounded.

> That was so powerful and moving! Truly magnificent! I can't believe the impact on them, and on me.

Singers Take the Stage

Why is all this important? Singers must identify the objective, the other, the story, the spark, and the stakes in order to have a reason to sing. Without these elements, they have no internal justification to "come onto the stage and stay there." With these elements, they have just as much purpose as those conservatory singers in the opera choruses. Again, this might seem like an inordinate amount of work, but it is actually simple and can be done with the speed of the imagination—almost instantly. When you try the upcoming "Happy Birthday" exercise, you will see how easy this actually is.

The Fourth Wall

One acting technique is particularly helpful for those singers who might be shy or self-conscious. The technique, called The Fourth Wall, gets its name from the traditional "box set" used in theatre in which there is a back wall and two side walls, but no front wall. (If it had one, it would obstruct the view of the stage.) Since the actors do everything they can to fill their heads with character thoughts so that they can live fully in the world of the play, one of the things they do is recreate this fourth wall. That way, when they look out toward the audience, their imagination leads them to "see" a tree, a clock, a valley—whatever might be on that plane between them and the audience if the fourth wall hadn't been "removed."

Singers can do this as well. If their imagination creates a very simple environment for the other, their belief in their story will strengthen appreciably. Using *Fair Phyllis I Saw,* let's see how this might work.

If we take the scenario in which the singer is in the barn, singing to someone they want to kiss, we can get the imagination rolling. The simple question we answer is, "What is immediately near and around the other?" In this case, we could say that the other is sitting on a ratty wool blanket, their back against a ten-foot-tall haystack. To their right, about two feet away, is an old pitchfork. To their immediate left is a leather harness for the mule. The key is that the singers make these surroundings "real" by specifying the concrete details. Colors, textures, flaws, sizes, smells, noises—any details that would support their story's environment would help the singer believe.

"Face" the Director

In order to maintain their belief in the other, singers can use their imaginations to create a specific other standing in front of them. If they don't, the fact that they are looking at the director while singing could destroy their connection. Luckily, the imagination is so powerful this need not happen. In fact, singers have the power to turn their director into a demon or a princess, a kindergartner or the president, a bird or a whale. When the choir faces the director—looking your way instead of at the audience or each other—you become the other in the singers' minds.

The singers can face you a couple of different ways.

- They can make you the other, creating a story that would incorporate the need to affect you. The story could be based totally or partially on truth, or be completely fictitious.

- They can imagine that you are the other, in much the same way that an actor believes that other actors are their characters and not the actors themselves.

- Using their imagination, they can create a very specific other which they then overlay onto your face.

- They can place the other's face right above or slightly to the side of your own. This way, they can still follow you (getting eye contact with you if necessary) without being distracted. This is especially helpful in the early stages of their "facial construction." Once their other is strong, they can shift that face over or onto your own.

If their story has them trying to affect the audience, you can remain the director in your singers' minds. If you are conducting them, wanting them to watch you and only you, the singers' objective can still be on affecting the audience—they just won't be able to look at them until after the song is over. The better alternative with such an interpretation is to either have them sing unconducted, or encourage them to make direct eye contact with many different audience members while keeping you in their peripheral vision. (If they do make eye contact with audience members, they should do so for no longer than 3 seconds per contact as that can make either party feel uncomfortable.)

♦ An Exercise for You and the Choir

The choir sings three versions of *Happy Birthday*. You conduct.

The first time, they pretend it's your birthday. Tell them to give you the gift of good phrasing, crisp consonants, matched vowels, tuning—all the technical elements you normally incorporate.

The second time, give them this story incorporating character, imagery, an objective, the other, high stakes, the spark, and obstacles.

> The person they sing to has just returned to the choir after a two month absence. They were in a near fatal accident that disfigured them, and were released from the hospital today. Every singer loves this person, but no one was able to visit them in the hospital because of critical family business. Now the person is back, standing in front of them for the first time since the tragedy. It's their birthday.

> The singers' objective is to make the person feel loved and treasured. The stakes are high because the person was so scarred that they now feel physically loathsome and unlovable, in part because none of the choir came to visit them. The singers' subtext might be, "You are beautiful. I love you so much, I'm so sorry I couldn't visit you, and I would be devastated if you hated yourself." The spark? The person looks at the singer and says, "Why didn't you come to visit me?"

After getting this information, the singers close their eyes for about 30 seconds and come up with their own specifics. Who is this person? What specific injuries did they incur? What do they look like now? Why do they love the person so much? When they sing to this person, they "face" you, using the method of their choice. They can each sing to a different person, real or fictional. One measure of their commitment to the process will be their reaction when they hear "Happy Birthday dear *JRAiesdoiufowieury*." If they crack a smile or lose intensity when they hear this mishmash of sound, they need to make their connection more specific, and raise the stakes, possibly giving themselves an obstacle at that exact moment. Ask them to do so, then try this version again.

For the third rendition, give the singers a different story.

> A good friend of theirs is despondent, having been betrayed by their (now former) partner. Not only was the cheating cruel and insensitive, so were the cheater's words. When this friend discovered

the betrayal, the cheater insulted, berated, ridiculed, and shamed them, all in front of the "new love." The friend hasn't been able to leave their house since, and breaks into sobs at the least provocation. The cheater now stands in front of the group, and hasn't a clue that everyone knows what they've done. *Happy Birthday.* (For young singers, try "Bully Puts Gum in Everyone's Hair...")

The singers come up with their own objective, high stakes, and subtext. What do they want the cheater to think, feel, or do? Are the stakes as high as they could be? How do they feel about the cheater right now? What specific message do the singers want the cheater to receive? This would be the subtext that probably differs from "I hope you're having a great birthday!" You might also have them sing "Lousy birthday to you..." so they can experience the difference between subtext and literal language. (Or, if they're mature enough, you might have them spell "happy" with a "cr.") Singers can explore the concept of obstacle by having the cheater react defiantly at some point in the song. The spark flares when the "birthday person" flips a flirty wink to the singer standing front row center.

After hearing this, the singers take 30 seconds to build the details. Who is the friend? How despondent are they? What does the cheater look like? What terrible things did the cheater say to their good friend? The singers "face" you again and sing.

At the end of these three explorations, ask them to share observations of their own process with the people near them. Once they've shared, lead a discussion, perhaps asking some of the following questions.

Questions for the Group

- What did you notice about your own process during the exercise?
- Did you feel different when you introduced the story and the concept of affecting the other? If so, how was the first rendition different than the other two? How was the second different from the third?
- How were your thoughts different?
- Was there any particular moment where your belief in the other was really strong? What was that like?
- Did you sing differently? How was the choir's sound affected?
- Did anybody connect with the obstacle? How did that impact you?

- How did you make the other person believable for yourself? Did you discover any techniques that worked for you better than others?

The Power of the Tools

When the choir sang *Happy Birthday* using story and other truthful connection techniques, you may have noticed that the sound changed dramatically. If they felt comfortable enough to risk vulnerability, the singers' connection gave them the power of human will and emotion, which they then expressed. They looked different, they felt different, and they sounded different. Your experience as you stood in front of them was probably different, too.

If *Happy Birthday* were to be performed in your next concert, you would use this as your starting point. First, you would choose the general interpretation and tone that best matches the composer's intent. During each and every rehearsal hence, the singers would strengthen their specific connections (with your help) while you concurrently guide them to shape and unify their sound.

When the Language is Foreign

> Americans are people who prefer the Continent to their own country, but refuse to learn its languages.
>
> Edward V. Lucas, "Wandering and Diversions," *The Continental Dictionary* (1926)

Latin, German, French, Spanish, Mandarin, Swahili, Hungarian, Russian. How many of us during one season have sung songs written in at least three different languages? The dilemma for singers in such situations is clear. If they want to connect to the texts, they need to know their meanings. The problem is that there are often so many words in so many unfamiliar languages, it would take a huge effort to learn the literal translations. Many singers have neither the time nor the intrinsic motivation to do this amount of work. What to do?

One of the "side-effects" of using the truthful connection process is that singers will learn foreign texts with greater ease since the meaning of the text is stressed from day one. If the singers can learn the text through this process or on their own, that's great. They can then connect as if they were singing the piece in their native language. For singers, there are few things so freeing as having the complete translation "in their bones."

The next option in terms of ease of connection is to learn some of the key words but be able to paraphrase the rest of the lines. Once they have their story, their imagery, and all the associated techniques, they can then make up the translation for specific words, as long as the general meaning is there.

The third option is less preferable, but it beats a complete lack of connection. When the singers don't know the piece well enough to paraphrase, but do know the overall meaning of the piece, they can let their imaginations create the meaning of every phrase. This is not as difficult as it might seem, since the music itself will give contextual clues. If singers use either of the two latter techniques, they can help themselves by using word stress and forceful articulation—which is what they would do if they actually knew the meaning of each word.

Helpful Communication

The director can help singers authentically connect by using certain phrases and avoiding others. The key is to pose questions and suggestions that will encourage the singers to build their internal truthful connection details. If the director focuses on the singers' inner process, the choir will have more external expression.

When trying to create an expressive choir, a director's first impulse might be to give an external or result-oriented direction like "Show it on your face!" or "Make the audience believe you!" This is counter-productive. If the singers think about showing it on their faces, their faces will reflect *that* thought and NOT the thoughts and feelings necessary to support the desired expression. If they try to make the audience believe them, the singers' story loses integrity—their other shifts to "the audience," and their objective becomes audience-based. They end up losing the very credibility the director is trying to create.

When we express ourselves in life, most of the time we don't think, "Hmmm. Not bad. But I need to look more loving!" Or, "Oh yeah. I'm supposed to look angry now." The exceptions occur when we try to manipulate others by getting them to believe a lie. But most liars are suspect, and most songs don't have that orientation! No, in our everyday lives we look a certain way because of a genuine inner experience. If a director uses external language to build the House of Connection, the singers' internal foundation will be quicksand. *Addressing their thoughts—not their faces—is the key.*

Let's look at some juxtaposed examples. The first of each pair models language that will benefit the singers; the second reveals language that will actually impede their growth as expressive artists.

- **Helpful:** How angry are you? Why? What's so important? Raise the stakes and make it CRITICAL to affect the other!
  Not helpful: Look angrier!

- **Helpful:** Create one loving image of your mother, using as many senses as possible. Feel her in your heart. Now, make sure she feels your love when you sing to her.
  Not helpful: Show the love on your faces.

- **Helpful:** Try flirting more with the other. Let them know that you find them incredibly attractive. Get them to notice you alone out of the whole group!
  Not helpful: Be sexy.

While the helpful comments might take a few more seconds, they will have the impact you want. The others will only confuse the singers, encouraging them to "indicate" feelings instead of actually experiencing them. You will end up spending much more time failing to get them to express when you could have efficiently guided them to a powerful connection and expression at the outset. The goal is to empower singers to express the truth of their connection, not encourage them to manipulate their faces so that they *appear* to be connecting truthfully. There is a HUGE difference. If you can help the singers stay on the path to truthful connection, their expression will follow, and audience members will be truly moved—as will be the singers.

> Just as "C" comes before "E," so does connection come before expression. *Connected singers will be Expressive singers.*

The House Is Taking Shape

You now have many of the tools, materials, and methods needed for building the House of Connection. The ground of safety has been prepared, enabling the singers to be vulnerable enough to risk wielding the necessary tools. The foundation of imagery and objectives is mixed and poured. The frame of the story, plot, and character is up, and the sheet rock of the other is attached with high quality drywall screws of obstacle, high stakes, and the other's reaction. The electricians have wired the structure with spark and subtext. The House is looking great, and beginning to function as it should.

8

Personal Matters

For deeper meaning, I like to have the student relate
the text to his own personal experience.

Oren Brown, Master Teacher in A *Spectrum of Voices*, Elizabeth Blades-Zeller (2002)

The questions which one asks oneself begin, at last, to illuminate
the world, and become one's key to the experience of others.

James Baldwin, Introduction, *Nobody Knows My Name* (1961)

Knowledge of the soul would unfailingly make us melancholy
if the pleasures of expression did not
keep us alert and of good cheer.

Thomas Mann, *Death in Venice*, Tr. H. T. Lowe-Porter (1903)

Singers often encounter opportunities to get personal—to either sing about specific aspects of themselves, or to relate their own experiences to lyrics that don't apply directly to them.

Let Your Light Shine

Using *This Little Light of Mine* as both a metaphor and an example, let's see how the basic process of Personalizing works. Here are the two verses we'll look at:

This Little Light of Mine
Traditional Spiritual

This little light of mine,
I'm gonna let it shine.
This little light of mine,
I'm gonna let it shine.
This little light of mine,
I'm gonna let it shine.
Let it shine,
Let it shine,
Let it shine.

Don't let Satan blow it out,
I'm gonna let it shine.
Don't let Satan blow it out,
I'm gonna let it shine.
Don't let Satan blow it out,
I'm gonna let it shine.
Let it shine,
Let it shine,
Let it shine.

Clearly, this spiritual refers to Jesus' admonition to live full lives, sharing our talents whenever possible. Using text analysis, we can readily identify "light" as a metaphor for "good works" or "talents used lovingly." The music is jubilant and optimistic, expressing the joy of living in this manner. The composer/lyricist also expresses a lot of conviction, aware of the "Satans" that can prevent us from living full lives, but shaking a fist of defiance in their direction.

For a singer to personalize this song, they first need to connect to the exact nature of their "light." What specific good works or talents are they going to let shine? It is not enough for them to identify these as their "goodness." They must know exactly what that "goodness" is. Using thoughts and imagery based on their own experience, they might picture themselves confronting bullies at school, consoling their grieving best friend, singing at convalescent hospitals, or working in the Peace Corps—anything they do (or want to do) that lets their light shine.

Once the singer personalizes their "light," they need to identify their own personal "Satans." Even if they don't believe in an actual Satan, they can relate to the principle of a negative power in their lives. What force gets in the way of their joyful expression of good works? Is it their tendency to spend too much time in front of the television? Is it their materialism, their concern with owning the latest technology rather than caring for their fellow humans? Is it their own inner critic that fills them with self-doubt, extinguishing their light whenever it starts to burn brightly? Is it all of the above? Whichever it might be, specific images and thoughts need to be there. Since the singer is personalizing, these don't have to be created as much in the imagination—they just need to be specified and refreshed, then brought to the forefront while singing.

Plumbing the Depths

Personalizing could be the plumbing in the House—all the pipes and joints of our interior lives and past experiences. As it is but one aspect, it is added to all the other tools and materials as the House of Connection is built.

With a song like *This Little Light of Mine*, the singer will get more intensity—more "water pressure," if you will—if their personalizing is as intimate as possible, and the stakes are as high as possible. The deeper the singers reach, the more intense the experience for both them and the audience. Choosing the "light" of "standing up to my boss when they bully me," a conviction deeply held but beset by "Satans of fear and self-doubt rooted in a verbally abusive childhood," for example, will provide both a connection and an emotional charge for the singer. This is but one instance in which personalizing will imbue the singing with power and poignancy.

Dare to Share

Please note that the singers should never be required to verbally share their personalizing; indeed, their desire to keep any connection details private must be honored. That having been said, to challenge them to connect I often exhort singers to "Dare to Share." When they do so, however, they share their personal connection through the music, not in a public testimonial.

The Whole Truth

This Little Light of Mine is a song most people can identify with. Most of us have some part of ourselves we want to actualize, some good work we want to do that will improve the world. But what do we do with lyrics that are difficult to relate to? How can a singer connect truthfully when they would never speak such lyrics or think such thoughts?

While some might have a hard time accepting this, all of us have a "dark side" as well as a "light side." Method acting theorists tell us that we are each capable of ALL human thoughts, feelings, and deeds—no matter how base or noble they might seem. Social psychologists say the same thing. The famous Zimbardo Prison Experiment at Stanford (1971)—in which ordinary students were divided into two psychologically equal groups of guards and prisoners then left to their own devices in a makeshift basement prison—confirms this. While the experiment was supposed to last two weeks, the researchers stopped it after six days because of the extreme sadomasochistic cruelty of the "guards" and the victimization of the "prisoners." (For more information, go to www.prisonexp.org.)

This experiment, like Golding's *Lord of the Flies*, suggests that we have every aspect of humanity inside us—from innocent purity to brutal corruption. Look at yourself. Have you had thoughts ranging from extreme violence to the gentlest kindness? Feelings of hate *and* feelings of love? Attitudes that ranged from euphoria about your God-given existence to dark depression about this cesspool of life? Haven't your deeds reflected this wonderful dichotomy as well? This boundless human potential within us is the well to tap when the lyrics seem esoteric or personally irrelevant.

Even if the singer thinks that they could never hold such thoughts or speak such words, some part of them could—unacknowledged though that part may be. That is the aspect to spotlight internally and investigate during rehearsals; that is the internal truth that will often connect the singer to a challenging text.

The Inner Pot of Gold

Look at the lyrics below. They're fairly extreme, and only the most pessimistic and depressed among us would identify with them 100%.

I'm Always Chasing Rainbows
Music by Harry Carroll, Words by Joseph McCarthy

I'm always chasing rainbows,
Watching clouds drifting by.
My schemes are just like all my dreams,
Ending in the sky.
Some fellows look and find the sunshine,
I always look and find the rain.
Some fellows make a winning sometime,
I never even make a gain.
I'm always chasing rainbows,
Waiting to find a little blue bird in vain.
Used by permission, Warner Bros. Publications

While very few of us can relate to "never" finding anything positive in our lives, most of us have felt this way at some point—and most of us feel this way about some aspect of our lives. The goal, then, is to look inside and find that part of our experience—minuscule though it might be—that is frustrating, depressing, or hopeless. Being self-aware helps us in this mission. However, even if they aren't normally so, singers can learn to be introspective through practice.

Looking inward, even the most successful person has difficulties in some area of their lives. For example:

- Being able to fully relax around members of the desired sex.
- Learning a new language.
- Managing credit.
- Dieting and exercising.
- Standing up for themselves in a tense and heated argument with their significant other.
- Forgiving themselves for their behavior in social situations.
- Stopping that abusive inner (or outer!) monologue about other drivers.
- Loving all people, regardless of their actions.
- Making it through even one day without some negative judgment.
- Maintaining a sense of perspective around career and family.

When the singer identifies their personal "rain," they can then build on it to create a framework for their connection. Let's look again at this particular song, adding the singer's inner monologue. Remember that the inner monologue, like the imagination, is much quicker than the spoken word.

I'm always chasing rainbows,

I'm constantly trying to be more forgiving of my words and actions when I'm around other people.

Watching clouds drifting by.

But when I try, I notice that I just can't do it—and I beat myself up even more. Like yesterday when I told Amy she looked good and she took it the wrong way. I could've punched myself in the gut! Wait... I did. What an idiot!

My schemes are just like all my dreams,

Every plan I have—the string around the finger, the "pizza if I'm good," the meditating...

Ending in the sky.

They all fail. Now I can't even look at string, the pizza, or my Buddha statue without hating myself.

Some fellows look and find the sunshine,

Jim and Annette don't have this problem, and they aren't perfect. They both said about ten idiotic things at dinner last week but just laughed it off, enjoying the humor of the situation.

I always look and find the rain.

I stupidly called Annette "Jeanette," and my whole evening was ruined.

Some fellows make a winning sometime,

Even Merzad—who has the worst case of "foot in mouth" disease—cuts himself some slack every once in a while.

I never even make a gain.

Not me. In fact, I get worse. Like last night when I sent that long email to Christina and completely alienated her. "Are you feeling all right?" she replied. What is wrong with me?!

I'm always chasing rainbows,

I keep hoping for that day when I stop beating myself up in social situations...

Waiting to find a little blue bird...

Waiting for that day when I can just be comfortable with myself...

In vain.

Oh, who am I kidding? It'll never happen. Gosh, that makes me sad.

Substitution

Personalizing can run through an entire piece, as shown above. It can also connect singers to isolated sections of pieces, and it can even work when the singers are singing as a character and not themselves. A particular type of personalizing called Substitution can be particularly helpful in these instances.

I once worked with a boys' choir of 10 to 12-year-olds who were rehearsing *Prepare Ye* from the musical *Godspell*. The text for this piece is "Prepare ye the way of the Lord," first sung by the character John the Baptist as a solo, then repeated by the choir for the duration. The director was planning to use the song as the concert opener, with the singers walking down the aisles as they entered. Prior to using substitution, their faces and voices were lifeless, unexcited, and uninspired. This is hardly surprising because few fifth grade boys have a profound connection to Jesus, and even those who do may be reluctant to share those feelings while singing. (Note: If you pick music that is difficult to relate to for whatever reason, plan for the additional work necessary to create a compelling connection.)

The story that we created had the boys being disciples who were trying to excite the audience about Jesus' imminent arrival. The audience was comprised of specific people they knew who would benefit greatly from taking Jesus into their lives. All that was well and good, but the boys were still not inspired. Why not? They found it very difficult to relate to Jesus as an icon, just as they found it difficult to relate to the greatness of his teachings, even when relating them to their own experiences.

What helped the boys feel what John the Baptist and the disciples would have felt—the awe and excitement that is clearly expressed in the music—was substituting a personal hero in Jesus' place.

> Imagine you are getting the crowd excited about Barry Bonds, or any other person you would be absolutely thrilled to meet. Take 15 seconds to think about that, then get your neighbor excited about it. Now, use the song to get the audience thrilled about it, too.

Once they did that, the difference was remarkable. They—their faces, voices, and bodies—sparkled with expression, as did the piece itself. I couldn't stop smiling as I watched those young boys so ecstatic about the imminent arrival of their own "substitute Jesus." Their next step was to remember that feeling, and sing the song again, seeing if they could be just as excited about Jesus. After all, their characters felt about Jesus what they felt about Barry Bonds. They succeeded at this for the most part, especially when they made Jesus' miracles specific, but many needed to remind themselves how excited they had been about Barry Bonds in order to reclaim the feeling. A similar process works for many: Use substitution during the moments prior to singing, then transfer the feelings to the literal/textual meaning right before you start to sing.

When using substitution, the ultimate goal is to personalize the concepts and emotions found in the song. It would be ideal (and most truthful) if, after using substitution successfully, singers would apply their feelings to the literal meaning. However, sometimes the literal meaning is so obscure or irrelevant that they need to make their substitution permanent. No problem. It's better for them to be connected in a personally relevant way—even if their connection is technically not 100% truthful—than for singers to be disconnected.

Expand Your Horizons Inward

Occasionally singers will relate to a text, but their intensity of feelings about the subject matter won't match that of the lyricist/composer. While the technique of substitution can work here, another type of personalizing is often more effective. This technique we'll call Expansion. Expansion is nothing more than taking one's usual feelings about the subject matter and "growing" them to fit. Let's see how this might work. The following poem is a favorite of choral composers.

Barter
Poem by Sara Teasdale

Life has loveliness to sell,
All beautiful and splendid things,
Blue waves whitened on a cliff,
Soaring fire that sways and sings,
And children's faces looking up
Holding wonder like a cup.

Life has loveliness to sell,
Music like a curve of gold,
Scent of pine trees in the rain,
Eyes that love you, arms that hold,
And for your spirit's still delight,
Holy thoughts that star the night.

Spend all you have for loveliness,
Buy it and never count the cost;
For one white singing hour of peace

Count many a year of strife well lost,
And for a breath of ecstasy
Give all you have been, or could be.

For singers to connect and express the depth of humanity in a piece like this, they must engage their own humanity, including their deepest senses of awe and gratitude. Some singers are more in touch with this spirituality than others, and some are more emotionally vulnerable so they can connect more easily. However, most singers can find what they need to sing this piece with beautiful expression—but they might have to reach beneath the surface.

Let's look at one of Teasdale's "beautiful and splendid things" through the eyes of a singer whose intensity of feelings differs from that of the poet. For the singer to get more in touch with their deeper selves, they can access their "inner witness," the part that watches and truly knows us as we fumble through our lives. For the sake of the dialogue, we'll call the singer Chora and her inner witness Spiri.

Blue waves whitened on a cliff

CHORA: I like the ocean, don't get me wrong. But when waves hit a cliff and turn white I just see it as "spray." I mean, I studied Physics in high school so I know what the water is doing when it hits the cliff. Sure, when the surf is high and the spray is big that's cool, but my heart doesn't go all tingly about it.

SPIRI: Close your eyes and picture yourself standing on a cliff. Nothing is in front of you except the ocean, spreading infinitely before you. Smell the salt air tinged with decaying seaweed, hear the rhythmic pounding and hissing of the waves and the seagulls overhead, sense the subterranean rumblings below your feet when the waves hit. Feel how small and insignificant you are compared to the vast power before you.

CHORA: O...K. I guess I'm with you. But I keep thinking about Ocean Spray cranberry juice and the shopping I have to do before dinner tonight.

SPIRI: What an awareness of your inner process! Refocus on the ocean before you. See the waves, the birds, the foam, the rocks below, the tide pools being washed with new surges of water with every pounding wave. Now think about the incredible mystery that created this ocean, this world, your phenomenal mind and senses that give you the power to behold all this.

CHORA: Wow. It's kind of amazing when you think about it.

SPIRI: Now you're onto something. Look again at the scene before you. Your heart is now open to the mystery and splendor of our world and your Life. Open your eyes. How do you feel?

CHORA: I feel like I've expanded somehow, like I'm more available to feel things at a deeper level. I think I know what Teasdale is talking about when she says that waves hitting a cliff are beautiful and splendid!

SPIRI: Yes, you've got it! Of course, you had it all along, you just needed a little guidance to take you from your surface level thinking to the depth below. Do you see why Teasdale values this feeling of "ecstacy" above all others? Do you see why she advocates our gratitude for life's "loveliness"?

CHORA: Yes, this feels great! It's like I've been on a vacation for a month and all my ordinary ways of looking at the world are gone. I don't take things for granted anymore. I'm now appreciating those sunsets, those tender moments when my kids are holding my hand as we walk the beaches of Maui, that fire that warms and crackles as it toasts our marshmallows. My mouth even waters when I think about that "phenomenal delicacy"! I mean, when you think about it, everything can be lovely. You know what I mean?

SPIRI: Yes. And now you know what Teasdale means. Now you're ready to sing.

CHORA: I can't wait!

SPIRI: Neither can I.

Most singers will be able to connect to intense and "sensitive" feelings like these, though a few may find it difficult to connect to anything even resembling spirituality. (Many cultures today deify Rational Materialism, making spiritual awareness particularly challenging.) Other singers may suppress the necessary sensitivity because they have learned that a guarded life is a less painful life. Again, the safe environment you create can help them—the more supportive the atmosphere, the more likely that even these singers will break through the barriers to their own rich humanness.

Here are the steps that can lead the singer inward.

1. Determine the composer/lyricist's feelings about the subject matter.

2. Describe the music itself with adjectives like light, dark, sad, joyful, reflective, irreverent, upbeat, humorous, tender, angry, mystical, or bombastic. Check to see if the tone of the music supports the text. If the two don't match, see if you can ascertain why as this will give

you major clues about the composer's attitude. (When music and text are out of sync, look first for satire or humor.)

3. Once you determine the composer/lyricist's viewpoint towards the subject matter, compare it to your own. If your feelings about the subject are less intense, you're ready to go inward.

4. Identify the images within the subject matter, then get concrete and specific about them. Use all seven senses as you flesh out the imagery. Close your eyes as you do this so as to be less distracted by your surroundings. As the images you are creating percolate in your mind, allow them to affect you. Be aware of any thoughts or judgments you have toward the images and let them go. Only by accepting them freely will they touch you at that deep level. If you don't know much about the subject, do research; see if you can find out why the composer/lyricist feels the way they do. Once you can empathize with the composer/lyricist's viewpoint, all you need to do is "think their thoughts" and you will be connecting at their level.

5. If your feelings now match those of the composer/lyricist, you are where you need to be. If your feelings are still less intense, answer this question: Is there something in my experience that has given me a similar feeling?

6. When you come up with your answer, flesh it out in sensory detail. You will start to feel those feelings. Reconnect now to the images you created about the subject matter. Let your emotions guide you to empathize with the composer/lyricist's intensity.

7. Continue to flesh out the song's imagery. The more available you are to the "Specifics of the Seven Senses," the more intensely you will feel.

The Religion Issue

Those singers who find it challenging to experience their own spirituality might have no trouble at all with religion; when texts are based on the Bible, for example, they might be able to connect immediately. On the other hand, singers who are deeply spiritual might have difficulty with religious texts. Atheism, Buddhism, Christianity, Judaism, Hinduism, Islam—these are but a few of the names given to the world's thousands of religious belief systems. Chances are that your choir (even if it's a church choir) will consist of members who have many different thoughts and feelings about God—religion is a profoundly personal issue. Regardless, since so much of choral music is religiously oriented, it is vital that you have the ability to help ALL singers connect to "God."

The following suggestions apply to all singers, regardless of their specific beliefs.

- **Appreciate the Great Unknown.** Encourage the singers to expand their curiosity and sense of wonder about the world and about life. Ask them to use their senses of Awe and Gratitude whenever possible. The more they embrace the Mystery, the more they will come to know their own spirituality. Even if the singer doesn't believe in God per se, a connection to a Force Greater than Themselves can come from this spiritual awareness.

- **Believe in Some Notion of God.** It is not important that the singer believe in the God of the text—only that, when they sing, they believe in a God of their choosing. The belief is what's important, not the specific nature of that belief. One singer's amorphous "Great Creator of the Redwoods" can be just as compelling as another singer's anthropomorphic God who sits on a throne in Heaven. In the choral world, there is no "right" or "wrong" religious belief when it comes to authentic connection.

- **Create a Character Who Believes,** whose belief system mirrors that in the text. Encourage the singers to get specific and concrete. If they are singing a Buddhist text and they are Christian, it would behoove them (with your help) to know enough about Buddhism to be able to think what a Buddhist might be thinking. If the character advocates Non Attachment, the singer would know exactly what and how important that is, and could then connect to those thoughts when they sing. The great philosopher Descartes said, "I think, therefore I am." Ralph Waldo Emerson, in his essay entitled "Spiritual Laws," wrote, "To think is to act." If the singer thinks the thoughts of a believer, in that moment of singing, they believe. The singer, using the techniques of truthful connection, becomes a believer during that particular song.

- **Substitute a Person for God.** Many religions support the notion that God is inside us all.

- **Believe that God is Love.** They would then substitute their feelings about love for God. If the text supports this interpretation, the Bible and other holy texts support it as well.

- **Make Believe You're a Believer.** The singer would accept the fact that there may be a God and buy into it completely while they sing. They would then sing as themselves, but use expansion to amplify their own spirituality or open-mindedness to an actual belief in God for the duration of the song.

- Regardless of how the singer connects to God, they also need to **Create the Story and an Other** to support a compelling scenario for their singing. In cases where a singer just can't embrace the notion of God, they can use the other tools for truthful connection to give themselves an engaging purpose for singing.

Plunge Your Self Into the Text

Whether the singer establishes a personal connection throughout the song, or just with key words or phrases, this "plumbing" is one of the major elements of the House of Connection. As Hal David wrote, "A house is not a home when there's no one there..." Personalizing puts the singer "there" in a very tangible way, and can inspire and connect at the deepest levels.

9

That's Nonsense

To appreciate nonsense requires a serious interest in life.
Gelett Burgess, "The Sense of Humor," *The Romance of the Commonplace* (1916)

Do-be-do-be-do.
Frank Sinatra, *Strangers in the Night* (1966)

Singers have the opportunity to make an authentic personal connection when the text is full of meaning; they have that same opportunity when the text is gibberish. Singers connected to gibberish can delight and move their audiences. Singers disconnected from gibberish will lose that opportunity.

So, how does a singer make sense out of "Fa, la, la," "Ching-a-ring chaw," or "Sssssss (STOMP) (CLAP), fffff (SNAP) T"?

Engage Your Sense of Fun (the Critical 8th Sense?)

Since many songs using gibberish as part of their text are light and joyful, it often behooves the singers to enjoy themselves. Simply having fun with the musical interplay, rhythm, or nonsense syllables for their own sake can be a start. This is certainly true in many madrigals, but also true in vocal jazz riffs, where the "scatting" often has a life of its own—enjoyed and created for its unique expressive possibilities.

Make Sense of the Nonsense

A "fa, la, la" or "pum, pum, pum" could be a restatement of part of the text, or it could be an iteration of the singer's feelings about those words. Thomas Morley's lyrics at the beginning of *My Bonny Lass* give us a good example.

My bonny lass she smileth,
When she my heart beguileth,

Fa la la la la la la la la la la,
Yesterday in the tavern, I could have died when she saw me gazing at her.

Fa la la la la,
Ah, she is so beautiful!

Fa la la la la la.
But when our eyes met, she suddenly beamed, as if she were a fox and I were a rabbit trapped by her gaze. Yikes!

If singers use imagery, connecting to thoughts and feelings related to the text, their gibberish will have meaning, connection, and expression. This is particularly intriguing for audience members since they don't know exactly what the singers are thinking, but they can tell that a potent connection is taking place.

Talk Turkey

Many songs give singers the opportunity to make animal sounds. *The Little White Hen* by Antonio Scandello, for example, has "Ka ka ka ka ka ka nay" as a recurring phrase. Each time they "cluck" it, the singers exhort the other to "hear her cackle call" when the hen lays an egg. This is a great chance for the singers to enjoy themselves while they think the chicken's character thoughts. The more specific they are with the subtext, the more fun they and the audience will have. Creating specific sensory details would add to the merriment.

Ka ka ka ka ka ka ka nay, ka ka nay, ka ka ka ka nay...
There's that feeling again! What IS it?! Oh my gosh, it hurts...
(As the egg is emerging...)

Ka ka nay
PHEW! Now, what WAS that?
(Upon delivery.)

Ka ka ka ka nay, ka ka nay...
Hey! It's happening again! Wait... What is THAT feeling...?

Get Serious

The subtext for *The Little White Hen* fits the feel of the song itself—silly, light, playful, fun. If the song is serious, the subtext must be also.

In the dramatic composition, *The Boy Who Picked Up His Feet to Fly*, Joshua Shank embellishes Mark Robinson's text with several gibberish elements representing bird sounds, wind, and the main character's thoughts and feelings. In one compelling, frantic and dissonant section, Shank uses "la, la, la..." to express a young boy's horror at not being able to come back down to earth. In such a section, the singers would need to have an equally dramatic subtext with very high stakes. "Something's wrong! What's going on?! I should be descending! WHAT'S HAPPENING TO ME?!" would be a fitting subtext made even more affecting when combined with specific imagery.

Composer Libby Larsen has written a haunting and powerful women's piece called *The Womanly Song of God*, an affecting anthem to both women in general, and women who sing. While it's based on a meaningful text by Catherine de Vinck, Larsen has added a rich density of gibberish elements. In fact, more of the piece is gibberish than actual words. In this piece, Larsen presents singers with an opportunity to connect to their power and Godly beauty while singing long percussive phrases of "Dō dee Dō" and "Dō dih-gih dig-gih dah." During this gibberish, a subtext restating some of the lyrics would serve the spirit of the text and music. An example might be:

I am the power of life itself, the grace of the sea. Listen to me, watch me as I dance through life. Honor my female form.

Just as this restatement of text would connect the singer, so would personalizing—she could connect to her own determination to be respected in this culture.

I feel like my soul shrinks when men stare at me as I walk to work. I can't stand that! I deserve to be honored and respected as a woman!

Such thoughts would be far less eloquent than de Vinck's text, but they would still serve the humanity of the piece.

When they sing "La, la, la…" or "Dih-gih dig-gih dah," singers can connect to actual thoughts and feelings.

Use Subtext to Affect the Other

Just as subtext and its related feelings can connect the singer during gibberish, so can creating a subtext that they use to affect the other. For illustration, let's consider the text of a the Quaker folk song as arranged by Neil Ginsberg, *How can I keep from singing?* Our story has the singer trying to get a friend to stop thinking of themselves as a victim—to look instead at life as being grounded in an infinite and eternal creative force. The song begins with gibberish.

Oo Oo Ah Ah Oo Oo Ah Oo Oo Oo

I love you, sweetie. I feel so badly that you are going through such pain. But you don't have to feel this way. Listen.

My life flows on in endless song,
Above the earth's lamentation.
I hear the real, though far off song,
That hails a new creation.

No storm can shake my inmost calm
While to the rock I'm clinging.

It sounds an echo in my soul.
How can I keep from singing?

What though the tempest round me roars
I know the truth, it liveth.
What though the darkness round me close,
Songs in the night it giveth.

When tyrants tremble, sick with fear
And hear their death knells ringing.
When friends rejoice both far and near,
How can I keep from singing.

In prison cell and dungeon vile
Our thoughts to them are winging.
When friends by shame are undefiled,
How can I keep from singing?

Creating a specific subtext like this will not only connect the singer to the meaningless text, it will maintain their connection until the text is meaningful.

Finding Your Groove Is Instrumental

Many songs use the human voice to emulate the sound of instruments. For an example, look no further than the second of Debussy's *Trois Chansons, Quant jai ouy le Tabourin,* in which the choir "sings" a guitar accompaniment behind the mezzo soprano soloist.

In such cases, it helps for singers to find their "groove," that inner pulsing enjoyment of the music they are "playing." To assist them in doing this, you might suggest they mime playing their instruments or "move to the groove" during one or two rehearsals of the piece.

In addition, singers portraying instruments can tune in to the emotional tone of the music, whether it is communicated through words or "instruments" alone. The easiest way to do this when other sections or soloists are singing *words* is to create a truthful connection to those same words, using all the techniques at their disposal. If *everybody* is emulating instruments, the singer can create a story that will fit and be supported by the music alone. If they create a story with plot, characters, objectives, and the other while they sing, their connection will have meaning. This is tantamount to creating a film from the score—a great opportunity to engage the imagination.

Rock It Man

When gibberish signifies the forces of either nature or mankind, the singer can connect to the tone of the music and the composer/lyricist's theme. Let's say the meaning of the piece is, "How sad that humans never appreciate how much they are truly loved." The gibberish elements are warm rain bouncing off the roof of a house ("Sss puh tih sss tih puh...") and the engine of a generator creating "false" light ("RRR chukachuka RRR chukachuka..."). The singers' inner monologue during this gibberish could be "How sad. So much love down the drain. So many lives left unhappy when they could be blessed by loving friends. How tragic are our efforts to be emotionally independent."

No Sense? Nonsense!

Choral compositions and arrangements are full of nonsense, so singers have many opportunities to bring meaning to gibberish elements. When they succeed, they bring a continuity of connection that keeps them and the audience engaged.

> Yabba, dabba, doo!
> Fred Flintstone, 1,000,040 B.C.

10
When the Music Changes

Change as change is mere flux and lapse; it insults intelligence.
Genuinely to know is to grasp a permanent end
that realizes itself through changes.

John Dewey, *The Influence of Darwinism on Philosophy* (1909)

When old words die out on the tongue,
New melodies break forth from the heart;
And where the old tracks are lost,
New country is revealed with its wonders.

Rabindranath Tagore, *Gitanjali* (1912)

All the previous techniques support singers as they engage in the most important task of all—motivating musical changes. If the singers are only singing louder, slower, faster, softer because you are *directing* them to do so, their connection is not yet as fulfilling as it could be.

Interior Motivation

Let's look again at the "Composer as Architect" model. When the composer writes "*ff*" or "*pp*," "Mysterious," or "*legato*," they are giving us a technical external symbol for a human internal process. Sure, the composer wants the sopranos to sing the last "alleluia" *fortissimo*, but there is something guiding that composer to create the blueprint that requires such an outburst. The composer is connecting to and describing some aspect of human experience that then shows up as dynamics or tempo shifts. Therefore, as the singers build their House of Connection, they have the opportunity to connect to a similar internal process; they can make tangible and human what the composer only represented on paper. They can find a way to live fully in the music, to be permanent and viable residents whose connection enables them to live and breathe with the music. To do this, they must flesh out character and story, but also create the necessary motivation—the interior decorating, if you will—that will support the musical changes of each song. In short, the singers' connection is buoyed immeasurably if they have an interior reason to sing that last "alleluia" *fortissimo*.

Motivating Musical Changes

Here is but a taste of the variety of musical changes.

Softer.................Louder
Faster.................Slower
Tension.............Resolution
Crescendo...........Decrescendo
Legato................Staccato
Dissonance..........Harmony
Ascending pitch...Descending pitch
Key....................Change

Keeping the following questions in mind will guide singers to their critical connections as the music changes...

1. Is the character undergoing a particular change? Are they thinking something different? Feeling something different?

2. Are the character's feelings intensifying? Are they becoming more determined? More angry? More loving? More sad? More bitter? More excited? More joyful?

3. Does the word the character is singing correspond ordinarily to any particular emotional state?

4. Is the plot shifting? Is there a new element introduced? Does the music change with the action described?

5. Is the character's objective changing?

6. Is the level of conflict changing? Is the other acting differently?

7. Is the imagery changing? Is it more tender? More dramatic? More intense?

8. Is the composer/lyricist repeating a musical or textual element?

9. Is there an element of suspense, surprise, or shock in the text?

10. Are the verbs changing? Does it shift from "I *shout*" to "I *sigh*"?

11. Is there "word painting" going on, in which the music matches the meaning of the text?

To investigate this concept of interior motivation for musical changes further, let's see how it might apply to *The Boy Who Picked Up His Feet to Fly*.

First the text...

The Boy Who Picked Up His Feet to Fly
Music by Joshua Shank, Text by Mark Robinson

Soaring and spinning and touching the sky
The boy who picked up his feet to fly
"Hooray!"
"Oh dear!"
"So long, good-bye!"
Said Johnny and Jenny and Alison Bly

Flying on sunbeams and kissing the sky
The houses and trees all whizzing right by
As further
And faster
He flew upon high
The boy who picked up his feet to fly

Mountains and deserts and oceans and sky
The moon and the sun and the birds that cry
"No more,
I'm tired.
I've had my try."
Said the boy who picked up his feet to fly

The boy who picked up his feet to fly
Never was able to step from the sky
But flew on and on as years passed by
And deep in the wind you can still hear him sigh...

Now we're ready for the story, to be invented by the singer (from here on referred to in first person).

The Other: I am communicating with my nephew David, a bright and precocious sixth grader who is stuffing his resume so that he will get into Harvard. He's taking violin and voice lessons, studying karate, playing goalie on his school's soccer team, acting in the school play, presiding over his church's youth leadership program, and getting straight A's.

The Spark: While sitting around a fire on a camping trip with the singer's family, David has just announced that he is going to become a paperboy. "Because the publisher is promising a prestigious six day educational tour of ancient Mayan ruins to the newsie who delivers the most papers," he explains, "And this will look great to Harvard admissions!"

The Stakes: David is showing signs of severe stress. He flies into rages, alienates his peers on a daily basis, and yells at his parents whenever they ask him to help around the house. Clearly, he is in over his head and could suffer the rest of his life if he doesn't stop his cycle of over-achievement.

The Objective is to get my nephew to realize the damaging repercussions of his "wanting to fly so high" and change his behavior, so that he will be able to enjoy his life.

One Obstacle is David's own ambition—while I start to present this important lesson, David pulls out his French/English study journal and begins to conjugate the verb, *avoir* (to have). The second obstacle is his sense of autonomy—I must be careful not to alienate him. If David thinks I'm telling him what to do, all is for naught.

Imagery: "Johnny and Jenny and Alison Bly" are David's young neighbors—he used to spend time with them until his behavior became so unpleasant that Mrs. Bly asked him not to come around anymore. I, as the singer, know exactly what the Bly children look like. I also use my imagination to create images of the mountains, deserts, and various other sights that David sees as he flies.

The Plot: The fabricated fable of the flying boy was "made up" by me as a customized moral lesson for young David, but it does have its structure nonetheless.

> A young boy picks up his feet and flies. He soars and spins, seeing houses, trees, deserts, the sun, and the birds that cry. As the birds cry, the boy realizes he is tired of flying and wants to come down. But he can't, so he flies on and on and is flying still.

And now the music...

The complete score of *The Boy Who Picked Up His Feet to Fly* is included here for reference. Following the score is an analysis of our hypothetical singer's inner monologue. These thought and feelings provide the necessary support for the dynamic, rhythmic, melodic, and textual changes throughout the piece.

The Boy Who Picked Up His Feet to Fly

Mark Robinson

Joshua Shank

....23

Lightly, with warmth (♩.=70)

high____ The boy who picked up his feet to fly____

high____ The boy who picked up his____ feet to fly____

high____ The boy whopicked up his feet to fly____

high____ The boy who pickedup his____ feet to fly____

Lightly, with warmth (♩.=70)

𝄂ℰ𝒹. *until after choir comes in.*

24.... 28

piano tacet m. 29-31

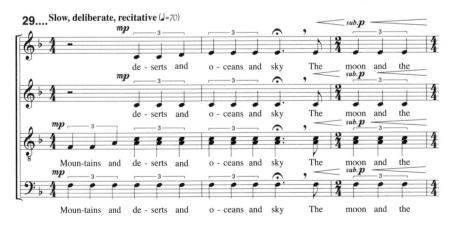

29....**Slow, deliberate, recitative** (♩=70)

de - serts and o - ceans and sky   The   moon and the

de - serts and o - ceans and sky   The   moon and the

Moun-tains and de - serts and o - ceans and sky   The   moon and the

Moun-tains and de - serts and o - ceans and sky   The   moon and the

* close immediately to "n"

** Soloists:

** Soloist:

46....

And deep in the wind you can still hear him sigh.

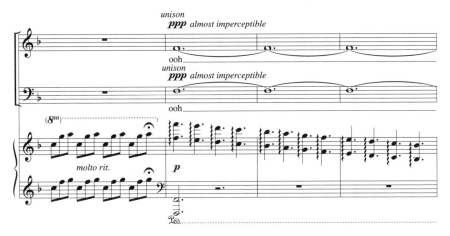

Matching Music and Meaning, Measure for Measure

The music and text of this composition have many elements that can support a singer's moment-to-moment connection. That connection, in turn, must support the music and text. Let's see how this process might work, from the perspective of the story above. (In this description, the singer's *subtext and inner monologue* will be in italics. The singer will be referred to in the first person.)

Reminder: The singer connecting to thoughts like these thinks more in pictures and feelings than actual words. If they do think "in words," the words flood their consciousness instantly, effortlessly creating their subtext and inner monologue.

Measures 1-5, page 123-124: To get David's attention, I accent the first syllable of the word, "Soaring." David looks up from his French practice, but then goes back to it immediately. I sing fully and *forte*, choosing my words carefully to interest him, but with no dissonance—I don't want to scare him or come off as too pushy. (Throughout the entire song I try to maintain a twinkle in my eye.) To reassure David and lull him into the lesson, I sing the descending melody of "How I wonder what you are" from *Twinkle, Twinkle Little Star* on "the boy who picked up his feet to fly." To get David's attention again, and start to get him intrigued, I (as a bass) add a glissando down to low F. He looks up and grins. *I have a chance here.*

Measures 6 thru 10, page 124: *Now I'm really going to grab his attention!* I sing the commanding interval of a fourth on "Hooray!" and then juxtapose it with the unexpected "Oh dear!" The reaction of the children concludes with "So long, goodbye." With the "Oh dear!" and the slight dissonance on "bye," I want to jar him a little and get him thinking about the down side of "the boy's" flying. *I can't wait for this next part.* When I sing "Said Johnny and Jenny and Alison Bly" I know I've hooked him—his grin of surprise and curiosity is unmistakable. *Yes!* The dissonant tension increases, to encourage him to consider the harmfulness of his own choices. *Is he thinking, "Hmmm... is this about me?"*

Measures 11 and 12, page 124: The accompaniment evokes a death knell, a somber tone. *Listen closely, David. Flying may not be as pretty as it looks.* I throw in the glissando to pique his symbolic awareness. *Will there be a tragedy here, David? Maybe, but it may be different than the one you expect.*

Measures 13 thru 18, page 125: I start singing *mezzo forte*, still wanting him to ponder the potential dark side of the boy's choice. *But I don't want to be* *too obvious.* So, I sing more about this "glorious" adventure of the flying boy, throwing in just enough dissonance to keep David guessing.

Measures 18 thru 23, page 125-126: To enhance David's reaction to the moral, I want him to empathize and enjoy this section. The more he gets emotionally and imaginatively connected here, the more power the lesson will have. I sing with excitement, wanting to "take him for a ride" with my voice and words. Word painting occurs in measure 19 when we vocally ascend as the boy flies "high." The tension is still there, subconsciously affecting him (I hope), but the sense is light and almost magical. The dissonance in measure 23 is more slyness on my part. Is the boy's trip magical and fun, or is there some sinister event to come?

Measures 24 thru 28, page 126: The music is almost hypnotic in the accompaniment here, gentle and repetitive. *See this boy flying, David. Imagine yourself up there, doing all those things you think you must do to be a success. Isn't this flying business grand?*

Measures 29 thru 34, page 126-127: The music is dense with harmony and pleasant dissonance—what a lovely seventh chord on "sky." *Ah, the journey! It seems ideal, doesn't it, David?* But the music gets denser, and its flirting with dissonance leads to harsh tone clusters on "cry." *That's right, David. The birds are crying, as will you be if you don't come down to earth. But I am too blatant. He's rolling his eyes. Time to back off a little and enchant him once more, this time with the hypnotic bird calls that still have that dissonant element, but are not so obviously didactic.*

Measures 36 thru 45, page 127-128: I re-engage David's imagination, getting him to see himself as the boy. *Yes, he dropped his French journal!* As I sing, "pum pum," I am both David and the birds, working until I'm beyond tired to maintain my impossible choices. I can relate this to my own life, as my family makes more demands on me than I can comfortably juggle with my business. Even this camping trip is stressful because I am losing time to prepare for Monday's meeting.

Measures 46 thru 52, page 129-130: I combine my own life frustrations with my hopes for David. These allow my energy to build and erupt on "No more," which is full of dissonance and longing. That longing and dissonance continues, with the basses and tenors carrying the longing and the sopranos and altos adding the tinge of dissonant pain. The boy is exhausted, singing *mezzo forte* after his initial outburst of "No more." He sings to David through me. I want David to feel the boy's pain and acknowledge his own—and I use my own experience as a grounding catalyst. *Is that a glistening I see in David's eye?* For the crescendo of measure 50, I (soprano or alto) think about

David's life and what it will look like even in a few months if he keeps it up. *How terrible! This is no way to live your life!* is my subtext for "ah." My own experience bolsters my conviction and supports the crescendo (soprano or alto) and the dissonance and accent on the word "fly" (bass or tenor).

Measures 53 thru 63, page 130-131: This frantic and dissonant section of "la's" juxtaposed with "fly" has my subtext relating to both "the narrator" and the character. The boy is communicating, *"Oh, this is terrible! I want to get down! I'm scared! HELP!"* I am communicating, *"David, do you see? Do you see how damaging your blind ambition is? It's awful! You're miserable!"* Finally, on measure 63, the tension resolves, giving David a chance to look at where he/the boy has been. *Look at it with new eyes, David.*

Measures 64 thru 68, page 131-132: Now I pose the question directly to David. The music is full of dissonance that supports my feelings about his choices. "Won't you come fly?" is a thinly veiled challenge to him: *"David, is this what you want?! Is this how you want to live your life?"* Finally, I'm done. I'm through with the heavy-handed and not so subtle symbolism. I back off now, as the dissonant energy clears on measure 68.

Measures 69 thru 94, page 132-134: The music becomes much calmer, slowing down to a repetition that invites reflection. The lyrics are sung very softly. *It's really your decision, David. Think about it. You go through all this trouble to "reach" some level of excellence, your life is awful, and then you "make it." You're at Harvard. Everyone shuns you. You have no friends, and you slip into a desperate lethargy. Your family is bruised and battered, feeling like they don't even know you. What is it all for?* On the last "ooh," I look at him and let him know, clearly, that I love him and want what's best for him. Only he can choose. *What will you do, David?*

Repetition

> What so tedious as a twice-told tale?
> Homer, *Odyssey* (9ᵗʰ C. B.C.)

The Boy Who Picked Up His Feet to Fly includes many text and music elements that illustrate the process of music matching meaning. There are several, however, that we need to discuss at greater length. One of these is Repetition.

When a text element—be it a word or a phrase—repeats itself, the singer's connection must justify that repetition. Why are they saying it again? What interior motivation do they have to repeat it? Usually it can be a matter of emotional intensity. As the singer repeats the element, their connection becomes more or less intense—but for a reason. The music will help the singers decide the exact nature of their different connections. Religious music, especially, gives us a wealth of opportunities to justify repeated elements, whether they be "Agnus dei," "Amen," or "Praise the Lord!"

Let's say the singer is singing the *Kyrie* from the Roman Catholic Mass, with the words *"Kyrie eleison, Christe eleison, Kyrie eleison"* ("Lord have mercy, Christ have mercy, Lord have mercy") repeated throughout the song in straight succession. The music is modern, dramatic, full of tension and power. For our purposes, let's say that this *Kyrie* starts *ppp* and builds to *ff*. Here are some inner monologues motivating the repetition.

Kyrie eleison, Christe eleison, Kyrie eleison *(ppp to pp)*

Lord, I am deeply ashamed. I broke my mother's heart when I left home so early, never to return. Christ, please help me forgive myself. Lord, have mercy—I am in voiceless agony.

Kyrie eleison, Christe eleison, Kyrie eleison *(pp to p)*

Lord, have mercy on the homeless. They live lives of such hardship and hunger. Christ, it frustrates me to think that our society can't do more for them. Lord, have mercy on them and help them find comfort.

Kyrie eleison, Christe eleison, Kyrie eleison *(p to mf)*

Lord, please forgive us our sins during this war. We have slaughtered tens of thousands of innocents. Christ, I'm so ashamed that we do this in your name. Lord, have mercy on their souls, and on the souls of their loved ones.

Kyrie eleison, Christe eleison, Kyrie eleison *(mf to f)*

Lord, have mercy on my friend, Rochelle. She is hurting so much from the stillbirth of her son. Christ, her mother just died, as well. She is in torment like I've never seen. Lord, please have mercy on her and relieve her suffering.

Kyrie eleison, Christe eleison, Kyrie eleison *(f to ff)*

Lord, have mercy on all victims of violent crimes. Christ, lessen the terror and unspeakable pain they feel.... Why do you allow this, Lord?! Have mercy on me for questioning your Divine Plan, but I'm so angry! Lord, have mercy and do more to help us STOP HURTING ONE ANOTHER!

When Singers Are Silent

Even connected singers often miss a great opportunity—maintaining connection when they are not singing. They might be silent at any time during the piece—either when their section is silent (while other sections are singing), during an instrumental interlude, or during the instrumental introduction or conclusion. While maintaining the connection during these times is challenging, the method of connection itself is easy and familiar.

When the singers are silent, they can maintain connection by keeping their inner monologue tied to the story, and their objectives tied to the other. Answering the following questions will help.

- What is the other doing in the silence?
- What are my images, thoughts, and feelings?
- What is happening in the story?
- What motivated me to stop singing, only to begin later?
- If someone else *is* singing, can I connect to their text?
- Am I trying to affect the other in the silence?

If the singers have yet to sing, they would know all the relevant details and images, including the fourth wall and the spark. What internal experience motivates them to begin singing? The music itself can act as the score, guiding their imagination as it creates imagery, thoughts, and feelings to match. If the introduction is somber and reflective, for example, the singers will be guided to a similar interior experience. During the organ introduction to an arrangement of *Ave Maria*, the singers might visualize Mary standing before them, let themselves be affected by her presence, and let her know how much they love her. To create high stakes, they can use imagery to connect to the reasons why they desperately need her loving care. If the silence is at the end of the song, similar principles apply. The important thing to remember is that singers can always be connected, even when they are not singing. If they stay connected, so will the audience.

Before the Downbeat

The time right before the downbeat also counts, and counts heavily. If singers are having difficulties with connection at this time, chances are they will continue to struggle throughout the song. When you raise your hands prior to the downbeat, look at the singers. Do they look alert, alive, purposeful—like they have something definite to say and they can't wait to sing? Do their faces reflect their specific connection to the upcoming song? If not, perhaps they have a generic expression, one that may be either excited or bored, but one that communicates "I'm waiting for the downbeat." Singers will have that expression if they're not connected and internally motivated to sing the very first words.

Here is a clear and compelling technique you can use to help them in this critical time: Place your hand over your heart before the downbeat. As you do this, you remind them to make their "heart" connection to the song. Your making this choice will profoundly impact the singers as they learn the craft of connection. If you do this consistently before you begin every song, you will make an invaluable contribution to the choir's culture of connection and charisma. I can't stress the importance of this enough. If you are in rehearsal, you have the advantage of being able to stop and remind them: "Do you have your story? Your character? Your other? Are your stakes high? Is your imagery specific?" In performance, placing your hand over your heart will say it all.

> The most important moment of any song
> Is the moment before the choir starts to sing.

When Singers Motivate Changes

As you guide and encourage them throughout the rehearsal process, the singers in your choir will create truthful connections, connections that will energize and motivate every moment of every song. They will experience and share more of themselves than ever before, and the music will be infused with their humanity and passion.

The Conclusion— A Beginning

I've been singing for 60 years and I have always had so many feelings I've wanted to include in my singing. These techniques have made that possible for the first time.

Workshop participant

I've always loved being in choirs that connected, but I never knew how to do it myself. When you think about it, that's what choir is—a choir is a group of people connecting.

Workshop participant

Many people join choirs, and for many reasons, but not all have had the experience of singing in "choirs that connected." That experience offers benefits like no other—it allows us to engage our limitless imagination, share our truest and deepest selves, and connect to each other through our shared humanness. Not a bad gig for the person lucky enough to sing in such a group. But luck shouldn't play a part here. Every choir can be "a group of people connecting."

I hope that *Choral Charisma* has been a source of enlightenment, amusement, and inspiration. If it serves your needs, or helps the singers in your choir, I am overjoyed. If it has presented food for thought, sample it often, but rest assured that you don't have to digest it—or incorporate the entirety of its principles—all at once. Use the techniques as you are inspired to do so, choir by choir, day by day, and song by song. The book is meant to be frequently picked up, thumbed through, and perused; a nibble here, a picnic there, and maybe even a feast every once in a while.

While the concepts may be unfamiliar, the more you incorporate them, the more familiar they will become. With practice will come proficiency. With proficiency will come ease. With ease will come expertise. (You will find *fun* wherever you are on this continuum.) This is not difficult stuff, when you examine it closely. After all, each of us is human and knows something about singing, and that is really the subject at hand—celebrating the human condition through song. With a little practice connecting to our personal and collective humanity while we sing, we will have new gifts to offer ourselves, each other, and our audiences. We'll also bring something new to the music.

Appendix One

Chapter Two Exercises

Safety, Vulnerability, and Commitment

With each exercise, the way you facilitate them is crucial. Here are some guidelines.

- Help the singers process their experience (either in small groups or large). "What did you notice about your own process? What was different this time?" Encourage them to use "I" and not "You" when they respond. This will bring them back to themselves, and help them realize that people have different experiences. This processing can be done any time you feel it's necessary, but works well at the end of each "round." Invite *volunteers* to share, and allow them to discuss only their own process, not thoughts about other individuals.

- Remind everyone of the importance of support. The way they support each other in these exercises will have a significant impact on their expression, and on their ability to trust one another and be trustworthy. Reinforce the notion that there is no "good or bad, right or wrong" way to do any of the exercises. They are all designed to help the participants explore process, both their own and the group's.

- Avoid singling anyone out when you make comments. Saying something like, "The whole group had more commitment, but Joanne still needs to work on it" is potentially shaming and not as supportive as saying, "The whole group had more commitment, and we still have room for growth. Fabulous!"

- If you're concerned that a particular singer really needs to "hear" the message or grasp a critical concept, you can do more exercises with the group. (The odds are good that others could also learn at a deeper level.) Checking for understanding and self-awareness is also helpful. Saying something like "How many of you notice that you get nervous when someone is watching you sing?" can give you a sense of whether or not individuals grasp their own particular needs. When all else fails and you just have to let an individual know that "you're talking to them," call for a slight break or create an assignment that will enable you to speak to that person without drawing attention.

- It's often valuable for you to restate content or reflect emotion after someone shares. The reflection can be as simple as "Wow! Exciting!" or as complex as "It sounds like you really overcame some obstacles and found your passion today. That is huge! Congratulations!"

- Challenge them to be aware of their own process, and to push past their own inhibitions so that they can be even more committed and "in the moment" the next time they do the exercise.

- Help them be aware and responsible for their own judgments. Depending on their maturity, you might inform them that we tend to judge people for qualities that we don't like in ourselves. "If you notice a judgment," it helps to say, "be aware of it, take responsibility for it, but don't act on it. Look inside and try to figure out how that person reminds you of a part of yourself that you don't like."

◆ Zip! Zap! Zop!

The purpose of the game is to introduce the concept of commitment and inhibition, and give the singers an opportunity for both self-awareness and group awareness.

The director and choir members stand in a circle (or circles if the group is bigger than 30). One person extends their arm straight out towards another singer, looks them steadily in the eye, and shouts (projects loudly), "Zip!" Whoever the person is pointing to "receives the energy," extends their arm toward another singer, looks them in the eye and shouts, "Zap!" That singer extends their arm and shouts, "Zop!" This continues until someone makes a mistake by saying a word out of order. Then, the whole group reaches in front of them and pulls an imaginary cord, making the sound of a klaxon horn ("Ah OOOOO Ga!"). And the game continues with the last person to get the energy starting it off with a "Zip!"

About the Exercise

- The game is meant to be fast and loud (but without vocal strain).

- The singers will have varying levels of commitment. You might need to model what total commitment is, then challenge them once more.

- Encourage them to get very specific about thowing the energy and sound "into the very soul" of their intended receiver.

- This is a good exercise to do early in the group formation process, or at the beginning of a retreat.

Questions for the Group

- On a scale of 1 to 10, how many felt that your commitment level was above 6? Above 8? Above 9?
- The Inner Critic questions. (page 44)
- What did the group energy feel like that time as compared to the first time we did it? Anybody notice a difference?
- How did you feel when the group energy was more completely committed?
- How does this relate to singing?" (They might say things like, "When you sing, you are passing energy, too," or "When each person fully commits, it makes a huge difference.")

◆ Bunny! Bunny! Bunny!

Similar to Zip! Zap! Zop!, the purpose of this game is to increase the opportunities to confront the inner critic.

The group stands in a circle again, but instead of one person sending and receiving the energy, this game has three people doing so, with one operating as the leader. Instead of saying zip, zap, or zop, "Bunny, (bunny, bunny.....)" is said as many times as the leader wants to. OK. Here's the skinny: The leader is the "inner ear" of the bunny, and cups both of their ears with their hands, making their ears "bigger." They then wiggle their hands. The person on the leader's right is the right "outer ear" of the bunny. They cup their right ear with their right hand, and wiggle that hand. The person to the left of the leader cups their left ear with their left hand and wiggles that hand. When the leader starts saying "Bunny, bunny...," the people representing the "outer ears" say it with them. So, you have three people all wiggling their "ears" and saying "Bunny, bunny, bunny..." (Some people find their inner critic very quickly here!) To send the energy, the leader extends both arms in front, hands palm to palm, and looks someone right in the eye when the last declarative "BUNNY!" is shouted. The receiver of the energy becomes the leader and the bunny's inner ears. The two people on their sides become the two outer ears. And the pattern is repeated for as long as you feel the singers are benefiting. Then stop, process, and play again.

About the Exercise

- The game is meant to be fast and loud (no vocal strain however).

- The singers will have varying levels of physical, vocal, and mental commitment. You might need to model what total commitment looks like, then challenge them once more.

- Encourage them to get very specific about what their arm does, where they look when they throw the energy, how they project their sound "into" their intended receiver.

- This is a good exercise to do early in the group formation process, or towards the beginning of a retreat. It's always good to "break them in" with Zip! Zap! Zop! first, however.

Questions for the Group

- On a scale of 1 to 10, how many felt that your commitment level was above 6? Above 8? Above 9?

- The Inner Critic questions. (page 44)

- What did the group energy feel like that time as compared to the first time we did it? Did anybody notice a difference?

- How did you feel when the group energy was more completely committed?

- How does this relate to singing?"

◆ Sound Ball

Long a staple of improvisational theatre, this activity ups the ante slightly in terms of commitment, risk, and expression. It also introduces the element of "trusting your creative process." (As a precursor, you might do a warm-up, in which you make silly sounds—animal or otherwise—and then have the group repeat them in unison.)

The group stands in a circle. One person starts, "throwing" a sound with their hands, arms, and/or body. However they throw the sound, they must make committed and steady eye contact with their intended receiver. The receiver repeats the sound, "catching" it with their hands/arms/body, then throws a new and different sound to somebody else. This is where trusting the creative process comes in, because the sound they throw is spontaneous and created in the moment. Encourage them to allow "nonsense" sounds and gibberish to "come out," and not words or animal sounds. If some singers do make those sounds, however, just ignore it or process it non-judgementally when the round is complete.

About the Exercise

- The game is meant to be fast and spontaneous.

- The singers will have varying levels of physical, vocal, and mental commitment. Their inner critic will often show up when the singers are called upon to "catch" and repeat a challenging sound that they fear they can't do "well."

- Encourage them to get very specific about the sound they "catch" and their intended receiver.

- This is a good exercise to do before the next two.

Questions for the Group

- On a scale of 1 to 10, how many felt that your commitment level was above 6? Above 8? Above 9?

- The Inner Critic questions. (page 44)

- How does this relate to rehearsing? Performing?

◆ Sound Transformation Circle

This is a very effective, instructive, and helpful exercise that puts the individual more in "the spotlight," requiring them to express themselves publicly for a longer period of time. The exercise does have an element of safety built in, however, that prevents it from being overwhelming. That safety element is the fact that everyone's eyes are closed when the individual is doing the expressing.

Here's how it works. Everyone stands (or sits) in a circle with one of their fists extending into the circle, arm bent 90 degrees at the elbow. All except one person have their eyes closed. The person with their eyes open is the first person to go. (If this were you, you could lead by example.) This person moves into the middle of the circle where they keep walking around, establishing and then repeating a random sound pattern. They continue to make the random sound pattern until they have a creative impulse to change it. They then let it change gradually, without intellectualizing or "forcing," until it evolves into a new random sound pattern that they like. When they find that pattern, they move toward someone in the circle and tap them gently on the fist. The person tapped then opens their eyes and makes the same sound pattern in unison with the person in the middle until they are confident that they have a close approximation of the pattern. They then move into the circle (their eyes are open, remember) and the former sound-maker sits in the vacated seat and closes their eyes. (Their fist is now down, not up.) This continues until all singers have been tapped. The last person to go does the sound transformation, but then ends the activity dramatically, with either a "bang" or a "whimper" of sound. Is this exercise risky? You bet! Are there opportunities for growth? Absolutely.

About the Exercise

- The possibilities for commitment and risk are endless. Volume? Pitch variation? Weird rhythm? Odd quality of voice? Yes, all these are possible territories for discovering self-expression and confronting inhibitions.

- Like in Sound Ball, some people's inner critic will tell them that they can't make the sound they are being given.

- There is a great opportunity here to help them be "OK" regardless of the nature of their expression.

- Encourage them to constantly push past their inner critic and explore "the edge" of spontaneous creative expression.

- It's helpful to demonstrate the difference between "pre-planning" the sound you are going to evolve to, and "allowing" the transformation to take place in the moment.

- This exercise begs for complete processing, then an immediate do-over. Lots of awareness of self-process will occur in the group.

Questions for the Group

- On a scale of 1 to 10, how many felt that your commitment level was above 6? Above 8? Above 9?

- The Inner Critic questions. (page 44)

- How many of you felt some moments where you were really present and connected, enjoying your commitment and creativity (being 'in the zone')? What was that like?

- What did you notice about your own experience as you listened to those people who seemed to commit 100%?

♦ Sound & Movement Transformation Circle

The purpose of this activity is to give the singers a huge opportunity to confront their inner critic, engage with full commitment, and explore the dynamic creative process.

This exercise is identical to the Sound Transformation Circle except for three key points: everyone's eyes are open, the random and repeated pattern now includes whole body movement in addition to sound, and the fists don't have to be held out. When the person in the middle has found a new sound and movement pattern that they like, they then move to someone on the edge of the circle, continuing the sound and action until the outside person joins in. The new person moves into the circle, letting the sound and movement evolve. The former person in the middle takes the place of the new person on the circle's edge. The last person does the dramatic "bang" or "whimper" ending. An alternative way to play is for the people watching to create a rhythm with their hands (Hit, hit, CLAP. Hit, hit, CLAP from Queen's *We Will Rock You* works very well). This "sound foundation" gives some people more of a sense of support, and gives them something to work either with or against as they create their choices.

Does the idea of one person repeating "wild and crazy" moves while making really bizarre sounds in front of the group seem scary? It actually is very scary to some people, and since that is the case, encourage everyone to participate, but tell them that they don't have to go if they feel they are too uncomfortable. They can still be a part of the activity, but they just cross their arms in front of their chest when the middle person comes to them. Though this activity can bring up a lot of anxiety, it is an extremely valuable exercise for anyone involved in artistic expression. People have learned a tremendous amount about themselves and their creative process from this activity, and grown as performers.

About the Exercise

- It's a great one to do at a retreat, but make sure that the atmosphere is well on its way to being supportive before you do it. It can be done in an unsupportive atmosphere, but then the focus needs to shift to the people on the outside of the circle more. (What must they do to support and be trustworthy for the person doing the risking?)

- As in the last two exercises, some people's inner critic will tell them that they can't do what they're being asked to do. Great opportunity here—full commitment is the goal, not perfection. The "You'll look like an idiot!" voice will also be in full evidence, thus affording another opportunity for the singers to confront it and grow.

- Encourage them to constantly push past their inner critic and explore "the edge" of spontaneous creative expression.

- This exercise also begs for complete processing, then an immediate do-over. Much awareness about their personal creative expression, and the forces that prevent it, will come from this discussion.

- On the second go-round, it's helpful to say something like, "This time let it all hang out. See what happens if you release all desires to control the outcome and just GO CRAZY! But remember, wherever your process takes you is great because that's what it's all about. Being aware of our process is really the ultimate goal here."

- This is NOT an exercise in "energy matching" or self-censorship. Be careful not to say anything that would imply that the singers should keep their energy within some "acceptable" boundary. When you process, avoid statements that make them feel that their exploration was somehow wrong because it was "too big," "too loud," or too "out there." In this exercise, such judgments have no place.

Questions for the Group

- On a scale of 1 to 10, how many felt that your commitment level was above 6? Above 8? Above 9?

- How many of you felt some moments where you were really present and connected, enjoying being "in the zone"? What was that like? The Inner Critic questions. (page 44)

- How have you grown through the process of engaging in these exercises?

◆ Emotional Symphony

This activity includes both risk and a feeling of safety. Its purpose is to help singers encounter the inner critic and push past it towards free expression. It also gives them an opportunity to work together, creating an "ensemble expression" of emotion.

Divide the group into three or four different "sections." (They should be in singing formation for this, but this could mean either a circle or other staging.) It would be interesting to experiment with different voicings (SATB, TTBB, SSAA, etc.), mixed groups (standing right, center, left). Once they've all done it twice, you could invite a quartet or trio to perform in front of the group. This brings a whole new level of risk and opportunity, so you might have everyone break up into trios or quartets for the culmination of this particular exercise.

Here's how it works. After getting some suggestions of "high energy emotions or states of mind" from the group, assign the different sections one emotion/state of mind each. The sopranos might get "rage," the tenors might be assigned "joy." They can only communicate these emotions with non-verbal sounds, no words. Any sound though, be it whimper, grunt, moan, roar, or "BaaAUREmmmGLPehnZ," would apply. As long as they relate it to the emotion and try to follow your conducting, the singers will all be aiming in the same direction. That's right, you get to conduct them. You can give the whole group a signal that means they're all "playing," or you can isolate different sections, having two or three "playing" at the same time. The possibilities and permutations are endless! It's also fun to pit one "against" the other, giving them a signal to turn towards each other and "fight it out." Besides determining who "plays" and when, your most important role is to give them lots of variety in the LEVELS of their emotional/mental state, from *pianissimo* to *fortissimo*, and many levels in between. (For emotion ideas, see page 161.)

The safety element here is that nobody is "playing a solo." The risky element is that nobody is doing the exact same thing at the same time, and there are many chances to "make fools" of themselves (aka "push their edges").

About the Exercise

- Encourage them to "go for it" and stay true to their connection while following the director.

- The first time they do it, just have them make the sounds. Give them no more guidance.

- The second time, have them think of something that really connects them to their particular emotion/mental state while they are "playing."

- Invite them to think of specifics—real people, real situations that correspond to the levels as well.

- Encourage them to notice their inner critic and their self-consciousness (hyper-awareness of others' opinions), and see if they can find ways to stay committed to their own connection and expression.

Questions for the Group

- Was anybody impacted by the energy of the others in the group? Did this make you commit more or less? Why do you think that was?

- The Inner Critic questions. (page 44)

- Did you notice a difference between the first and second times? What was one thing you did the second time that really made a difference? How does all this relate to singing in a choir?

Expression Exercises

Regardless of the reason for a singer's lack of expression, it is helpful for them to see and hear the difference between an expressive singer and an unexpressive singer. Their simple awareness will often serve as a catalyst and motivation for change.

The exercises below are designed to heighten awareness of expression and help singers understand its benefits. Some of the exercises will also educate them about their own strengths and weaknesses in this arena, so that they can then use that information as a starting point for their growth process.

◆ The Line of Expression

Whole rows of singers come to the front and sing. The watchers describe specifically and objectively what they notice about the faces and bodies of the singers, or the row could be silent and watch the choir sing.

These are *value-neutral* observations, used to take the possibility of judgment out of the exercise. Nothing is good or bad—it just "is." The observers' comments can apply to all the singers, not just the singers who are obviously expressive. The important safety elements here is that they do not name the singers, and their comments are without judgment—good or bad. Even after a careful explanation (including examples like the ones below) and some guided practice, the singers may still need careful coaching. As soon as you sense that their comment contains judgment, calmly stop them with something like, "Hold on. The word 'great' is value-laden. Try again, but just explain what you saw or heard, not what you felt about it."

The observers might say something like:

- I notice that some people don't move their heads at all, and some people move them quite a bit.

- I notice that I was drawn into the song when I watch the singers who look like they are sincere.

- I notice that some people seem to always have the same expression on their face.

Notice that anonymous and value-neutral feedback will not include statements like these:

- Some people are not very expressive.

- The three guys are doing an excellent job; I really believed them." (Even if the comment is a compliment, it still inserts the notion of "good and bad" into the exploration, and this can shut down people's willingness to risk. There is a place for value-laden feedback, but it comes later.)

This exercise and the next can be done with no processing. As they sing, simply have the singers emulate three expressive singers they see.

◆ The Circle of Expression

This could be a good first exercise to introduce the whole topic of expression, or it could be done at most any other time.

The singers stand in a big circle, with you conducting them from the middle of the circle. It can also work if they stand in two groups facing each other. They sing, and during their singing they notice the differences in expression and connection between different singers. During one of the rounds have them switch back and forth (on your cue) from "lots of expression" to "no expression. After they have processed their feedback, they do it again, this time trying to be as expressive as the most expressive person they see. Process their experiences. (It helps to pick a song or part of a song in which all are singing the same words at the same time.)

Questions for the Group

- What did you notice when you looked at different people? (Again, anonymous and value-neutral feedback recommended.)

- How were your feelings impacted by different people's levels of connection and expression?

- How were your thoughts affected?

- What did you notice about yourself when you sang with no expression versus lots of expression? What happened when everyone tried to match the most expressive singers?

Regardless of the song being sung, you might have them all sing it "with a frown," then all sing the same selection with the "jump-start" smile. Then ask questions like

- How was that? Was there a difference for you?
- How did you feel?
- What did you notice about the collective sound or listening experience?

◆ Partner Process

This exercise is most valuable once you and the singers have started to incorporate the truthful connection techniques.

Have the singers work with a partner, turning towards each other and singing part of a song. The entire group can sing at the same time, or you can ask half the group to sing while the other half watches. Stop them after 30 seconds or so, and ask them to tell their partners their experience of their own connection, each member of the partnership speaking while the other listens. After this report of individual process, give time for each person to give their partner feedback. Your guiding questions for these reports could be,

- What facial expressions did your partner have?
- When did you think they were the most connected? The least connected?
- Offer one thing that they might do to deepen connection or enhance expression.

Then, have everybody sing the same section again, and have the singers report on their own process, then have the partners give feedback, specifically focusing on differences or moments of increased connection.

◆ Mirror Work

Recommended material: A hand or pocket mirror for every singer. (Stored in a box and kept in the choir room, perhaps, but accessible.)

Working with mirrors can be extremely instructive for singers. At any point in the rehearsal process, you can say, "Take out your mirrors, everyone. It's time for an Expression Check." Have them hold the mirror up to their face so that they can see you and the mirror at the same time, then conduct them. After they have sung for what you deem "enough time," they give feedback to the person standing next to them about their own expression. The questions they address could be,

- When was I most expressive? Why?
- When was I least expressive? Why?
- What did my face do when I was the most expressive?
- What was my strongest moment of connection? How did I feel? What was I thinking?
- What were ALL the things that happened on my face when I sang with expression?
- What do I need to do to make all my moments as expressive and connected as my strongest moment?

◆ Adapt Your Warm-Ups

To keep daily focus on the truthful connection concepts, adapt them to your own warm-ups. Have the singers do their usual vocalises, but encourage their specific and concrete imaginations with suggestions like the following:

Sing this warm-up...

... to a sad kindergartner, trying to cheer them up.

... as if you were a teenager trying to get Mom to give you the car.

... to a roomful of scared children, trying to calm and reassure them.

... to your toddler, trying to get them to laugh.

... as if you were the president trying to win votes.

... to a mean person, stinging them with your rebuke.

... as if you were a holy person, giving someone their last rites.

... to your conception of God, asking for forgiveness.

... as if you were a spurned lover, pleading for another chance.

... to an associate, telling them a slightly naughty joke.

... as if you were a student, desperate for your study partner to clarify a concept before your final exam.

... to a teammate, after your team won the world championship.

... as if you just heard a juicy bit of gossip, and can't wait to share it.

... making up your own story and compelling reason to sing.

... making up a truthful emotional connection to the text.

... making up a specific other that does something to impact you in the midst of your singing.

As they do these, be aware of the completeness of their belief. Are they trying to "look like" they are feeling/thinking/doing something, or are they actually buying into the stories and engaging their imaginations? You will see a variety of levels of commitment and inhibition—asking the inner critic questions would be appropriate if necessary. As you do these, you will probably think of other stories and scenarios that will work with your favorite warm-ups. Have at it!

♦ Videotape and View

This exercise provides singers an opportunity to see their own expressiveness and compare it directly to that of other singers. It can be an extremely effective wake-up call and an excellent motivator.

Have someone videotape the singers during a rehearsal, panning the group very slowly and focusing on one face at a time. At certain points, the camera can zoom out to include more singers and get the "bigger picture." Give singers at least a few tools of connection prior to the filming so that their self-consciousness will be lessened.

When you show the tape, make sure the feedback will be supportive. Ask value-neutral questions like, "What were the qualities that the more expressive singers had?" or "What did you learn from this?" If you want the individuals to share their perceptions of themselves, have them team up with a partner with whom they share perceptions of their own strengths and opportunities.

♦ Examining Effective Expression

Pick a few singers who are obviously connected and expressive. They stand in front of the group and sing. Ask the choir to specifically and objectively describe what they notice, giving value-neutral feedback.

The comments might sound like these:

- Mary's head moved back and forth a little on certain words.
- Leroy's brows furrowed and his eyes looked like there was fire coming out of them on the word, "Beware!"
- On the word, "Alleluia!" the corners of his mouth and the corners of his eyes contracted.
- Their faces and bodies seemed always engaged—never casual or bored looking.
- I got a good feeling as I watched them.

◆ Expression Detective

During rehearsals, have singers leave the choir (one at a time) and come down to the audience position, where they then watch their peers' expressions. After observing for a certain amount of time, they go back to the choir and another person moves to the audience position. They could "just observe," noticing the difference in expressions and the way they felt when they watched different singers.

Or, they could place their "evidence" on an **Expression Chart,** on which each person records the number of singers they thought were authentically expressive. At the bottom of the daily column could be the choir's average for that day. This accomplishes several things. It keeps people thinking about expression, it gives the singers many chances to actually experience the difference between expressive and unexpressive singers, and it gives some idea of the group's process (and progress) as they move toward "whole choir expression."

This keeps everyone constantly aware of connection and expression, and helps combat the "We're too busy working on difficult music to even begin to think about such things" syndrome, which is actually counter-productive, and so dismissive of a choir's expressive potential.

◆ Expression Leaders

The following would be especially effective once the techniques de-scribed in the later chapters have been introduced.

Designate certain singers to act as "expression leaders," with each one be-ing responsible for a specific group of singers. Their responsibility would be to monitor the expressiveness of their charges, give them feedback, and work with them on improving their expression. (Because of this specific focus of concentration, it would be good to have the expression leaders and the section leaders be different people.) Obviously, the lead-ers would need to spend some time in front of the choir, but their doing so would not negatively affect the choral process. Just have them come down, one at a time, for three minutes or so during every rehearsal so they can observe their group, taking notes if necessary.

Whichever exercises you use with your choir, the important thing is that you integrate truthful connection work into your rehearsals on a regular, ongoing basis. Emotional vulnerability gives singers the ability to grow from this process, and your steadfast application of the principles involved will launch the choir to new heights of connection and expression. You might be surprised at how quickly they'll get there.

Appendix Two

Questions for Singers

Song Title _____

1. Could it make sense that you or your "character" are singing to some other? If so, who or what? In what context do you sing these words to them? What's your story? (This is created by your imagination if it's not obvious in the text.)

2. Why must you voice these words right now? (Create a COMPELLING reason. What is going on with the other—or within you—that creates this need?)

3. How are you trying to affect the other person/people? Does your objective change in different sections? On different words? (Be specific.)

4. How critical is it for you to get what you want? (The higher you raise the stakes, the more you will be able to connect deeply.)

5. Is there any imagery in the text (mentions of people, places, or things) for which you can create specific pictures in your head?

6. Are you allowing yourself to be affected by these images, by opening your heart to their beauty, horror, ugliness, humor? (If you don't feel affected by them, make them even more specific and vivid.)

7. Is there repetition of text? If so, what mental or emotional need makes you repeat yourself, and how is each repetition different?

8. Does the music change in pitch, tempo, volume? If so, what mental or emotional shift motivates you to sing louder or softer, faster or slower, higher or lower?

9. What is your connection to the subject? Is it as intense as the composer's? If not, how can you make it so?

10. Are you setting up your connection and story before the director gives the downbeat?

11. How do you keep your connection alive when you are not singing?

Connection Check: Are you connecting to every moment—with each word and note having its own power, meaning, and subtlety? Or do you find yourself singing large chunks of music with little or no sense of what you're singing about, or what it means to you or your character? Keep working to make every moment as strong and specific as possible.

As I Sing, I'm Feeling...

LOVE
Adoring Smitten Infatuated In love Loving Sweetness
Devoted Gracious Open Forgiving Caring Compassionate
Empathetic Sympathetic Merciful Kind Generous Helpful

JOY
Content Blissful At peace Glad Happy Joyful Giddy Excited
Proud Appreciative Thrilled Inspired Jubilant Victorious
At one with the universe Ecstatic Euphoric Overjoyed

CONCERN
Curious Worried Confused Perplexed Anxious Scared Frantic
Freaked out Overwhelmed Dismayed Terrified

AMAZEMENT
Shocked Incredulous Awestruck Enraptured

PLAYFULNESS
Funny Rambunctious Silly Flirtatious Bemused Amused
Tickled A twinkle in my eye Cute Like laughing

HUMILITY
Worthless Respectful Generous Helpful Congratulatory
Reverential Patriotic Worshipful

SADNESS
Disappointed Sad Depressed Regretful Sorrowful Nostalgiac
Longing Wistful Grieving Broken-hearted Despair

ENVY
Jealous Desiring Hungry Craving Coveting Lusting

DEVIOUSNESS
Conniving Manipulative Vengeful Underhanded

ANGER
Annoyed Frustrated Exasperated Critical Resentful Judgmental
Irritable Cantankerous Argumentative Angry Betrayed
Defiant Boiling Ticked off Furious Vengeful Rage

RIGHTEOUSNESS
Confident Determined Cocky Justified Smug
Powerful Pompous

To be handed out, or enlarged and posted for easy reference.

Bibliography

Blades-Zeller, Elizabeth. *A Spectrum of Voices: Prominent American Voice Teachers Discuss the Teaching of Singing.* The Scarecrow Press, Inc., 2002.

Barlett, John and Kaplan, Justin, editors. *Bartlett's Familiar Quotations* (Sixteenth Edition). Little Brown & Company, 1992.

De Bruhl, Marshall and Ehrlich, Eugene, editors. *The International Thesaurus of Quotations* (Second Edition). HarperPerennial, 1996.

Ekman, Paul. *Emotions Revealed: Recognizing Faces and Feelings to Improve Communication and Emotional Life.* Times Books, 2003.

Ekman, Paul. *Face to Face: The Science of Reading Faces* (A Conversation with Paul Ekman and Harry Kreisler as part of the Institute of International Studies' "Conversation with History" series). http://globetrotter.berkeley.edu/people4/Ekman/ekman-con0.html, January 14, 2004.

Ickes, William, editor. *Empathic Accuracy.* The Guilford Press, 1997.

Johnson, Steven. *Mind Wide Open: Your Brain and the Neuroscience of Everyday Life.* Scribner, 2004.

Johnson, Jeff. Video: *Ready, Set, Sing! Activating the Mind, Body, and Voice.* Santa Barbara Music Publishing, Inc., 2000.

Jordan, James. *The Musician's Soul.* GIA Publications, Inc., 1999.

Miller, Richard. *On the Art of Singing.* Oxford University Press, 1996.

Miller, Richard. *Solutions for Singers: Tools for Performers and Teachers.* Oxford University Press, 2004.

Newham, Paul. *Therapeutic Voicework: Principles and Practice for the Use of Singing as a Therapy.* Jessica Kingsley Publishers, 1998.

Stanton, Royal. *Steps to Singing for Voice Classes* (Third Edition). Waveland Press, Inc., 1983.

Thurman, Leon and Welch, Graham, Co-Editors. *Bodymind & Voice: Foundations of Voice Education* (A Revised Edition). The Voice Care Network, National Center for Voice & Speech, Fairview Voice Center, Centre for Advanced Studies in Music Education, 2000.

Permissions

Recommended Sources

Clark, Larry D. and McGaw, Charles. *Acting is Believing: A Basic Method* (Fifth Edition). Holt, Rinehart, and Winston, 1987.

Cohen, Robert. *Acting Power: An Introduction to Acting.* Mayfield Publishing Company, 1978.

Hagen, Uta with Frankel, Haskel. *Respect for Acting.* Macmillan Publishing Company, Inc., 1973.

Jones, Arthur C. *Wade in the Water: The Wisdom of the Spirituals.* Orbis Books, 1999.

Rockwood, Jerome. *The Craftsmen of Dionysus: An Approach to Acting.* Scott, Foresman and Company, 1966.

Stanislavski, Constantin translated by Hapgood, Elizabeth Reynolds. *An Actor Prepares* (Anniversary Edition). Theatre Arts Books: Robert M. Macgregor, 1948.

Quoted Authors & Experts

Index of Exercises

About the Author

Tom Carter's passion for the performing arts originated with singing. A great high school choral program kicked off his involvement, which then led to acting, stage directing, teaching, and more singing. He earned his BA in Drama Education and his English teaching credential from San Francisco State University, next joining the faculty at Ukiah High School. There he taught English and Drama and directed the drama program for four years. During the summers, Tom taught high school students at the Oregon Shakespeare Festival in Ashland, and studied acting at the Studio of the Actor's Space in New York. Tom's next move was to San José to enroll in the Masters program at San José State University and sing with the Choraliers. His Masters in Music Theatre supported his freelance theatre directing, which led to an eight year stint as artistic director of the Los Altos Youth Theatre, followed by an eight year tenure as teacher/director/department head at Woodside Priory School. Over his 30 year career, Tom has acted in or directed over 100 theatrical productions at all levels, has sung in numerous choirs, and has been blessed to work with thousands of students. He currently lives in Northern California, coaches choirs, teaches voice, and works as a guest clinician. To contact him, email tpcarter@earthlink.net or visit his website at www.choralcharisma.com.